wood art

innovative wood design

Gingko Press

First Published in the United States of America, September 2015
By Gingko Press under license with
Dalian University of Technology Press
Gingko Press, Inc.
1321 Fifth Street
Berkeley, CA 94710, USA
www.gingkopress.com
ISBN: 978-1-58423-543-9

© Dalian University of Technology Press
Address: Section B, Sic-Tech Building, No.80 Software
Park Road, Dalian, China
Tel: +86 411 84709043
Fax: +86 411 84709246
E-mail: designbookdutp@gmail.com
URL: http://www.dutp.cn

Contents

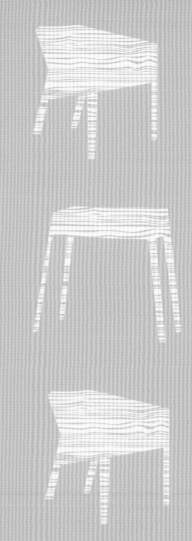

Furniture

My Writing Desk

NAME OF COMPANY | DESIGNER
ETC.ETC. | Inesa Malafej

This writing desk is designed to reduce the difficulties of working in a disheveled space. Storage space is organised around the tabletop which allows all items to remain in sight and are thus easily accessible. The entire surface of the desktop can be used without worrying that items might fall down; any unnecessary objects can simply be pushed to the storage sides. The high edges of the desk isolate it in room and create a positive microclimate and relationship with the user.

The wings are divided for simple constructions, leaving a path for wires. Additional features of the table include drawers for a laptop and writing instruments. For easier transportation, legs of the table can be twisted off.

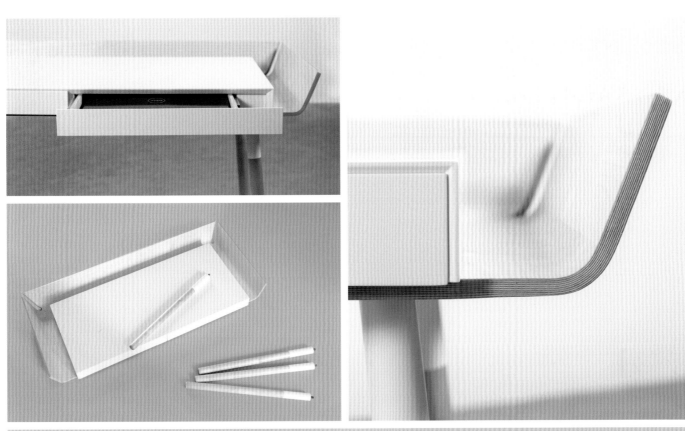

7

My Reading Chair

NAME OF COMPANY | DESIGNER
ETC.ETC. | Inesa Malafej

This armchair is comprised of two parts: the frame and the slipcover. The slipcover has multiple pockets that can be used to store books and other small items. You can also use it to keep your hands cozy and warm. The chair and slipcover allow various sitting positions for ultimate comfort. The slipcovers come in a variety of fabrics and colors that can be fitted to the frame of the chair, giving the user creative control of its appearance. This means the chair could wear anything from a modest suit to a leather jacket, adapting to any environment.

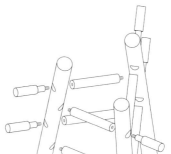

S02 Coat Rack

NAME OF COMPANY | DESIGNER
SmartwoodHouse | Zhao Lei

SPECIFICATION
W450mm × H1700mm

The S02 Coat Rack has a very simple appearance. Its beautiful geometry is formed by the interlocking round wood pieces, and different sizes of wood components are connected by hidden hardware joints. The coat racks are designed so they are easy to assemble and dissemble. Their honest design creates a clean aesthetic.

S03 Shelf

NAME OF COMPANY | DESIGNER
SmartwoodHouse | Zhao Lei

SPECIFICATION
D2040mm x W350mm x H1150mm

The S03 Shelf is a wooden shelving system, which can be assembled into shelves of any size and satisfy different spatial and functional requirements: decorative shelf, bookcase, room partition and so on. The S03 Shelf is assembled with seven building blocks, the pieces are well-designed so as to achieve the smallest flat-packing size, greatly reducing transportation costs.

"Lion Dancing" Folding Bench

NAME OF COMPANY | DESIGNER
CHU CHIH KANG SPACE DESIGN | Chih-kang Chu

This folding bench takes its inspiration from the concept of a standard flat bench used for sitting. The "Lion Dancing" bench is designed to 'sit up' and fold into two functional uses, thus reducing space requirements and conforming to the needs of the user. Wooden plates are jointed by "tendons" and only a steel axis is used for the folding function, which facilitates the fluency and durability of use. When folding, the bench can be formed into a six-foot shape, giving the body the appearance of a dancing lion.

A Matter of Taste

NAME OF COMPANY | DESIGNER
Tal Gur Design | Tal Gur

SPECIFICATION
D700mm × H700mm

PHOTOGRAPHER
Warhaftig Venizian Studio

Seven leading Israeli designers were invited to create an installation especially for an exhibition. The final results of this challenge reveal the thin line that separates "design" from "Art," which today, is in quick inclination to merge.

"A Matter of Taste" includes a modular table and three chairs, all made from plywood. Each unit of the modular table has six peripheral, hexagonal surfaces with a central one in a lower position, connected to a single leg. Fifteen such units show one of several possible combinations of a monumental table that relates to the specific space of the installation. The ergonometric seats have a rocking-chair base and a diagonal back that reaches far beyond the seat. The top of the chair is freely cut giving a haphazard appearance to the top portion. The seat itself resembles an open front box.

Little Angel Stool

NAME OF COMPANY | DESIGNER
Furf Design Studio | Rodrigo Brenner, Carlos
Eduardo Silva, Mauricio Noronha, Bruno Boas

SPECIFICATION
L300mm × D300mm × H650mm

For mothers who believe their children are little
angels.

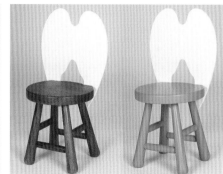

Verde Amarela Chair

NAME OF COMPANY | DESIGNER
Furf Design Studio | Rodrigo Brenner, Mauricio
Noronha, Bruno Boas

SPECIFICATION
L800mm × D800mm × H730mm

This is a chair inspired by the Brazilian culture.
Curves that only a Brazilian could have.

Monolog Bench

NAME OF COMPANY | DESIGNER
Tal Gur Design | Tal Gur

SPECIFICATION
D900mm × L2300mm × H900mm

PHOTOGRAPHER
Yigal Pardo

The bench and the side table designed by Tal Gur communicate with notions laid on the axis between mono block and monologue. The bench looks as if made from one piece – a tree trunk which fell or was chopped-off to which a straight multi-facets finish was added. In essence a mono block was transformed from being part of nature, as a tree, being inanimate as a bench. However, this tree trunk is not a mono block,

it is an assembly of wood boards to create the appearance of a mono block. Its edges are colored with an un-natural color for the inner part of the tree. It just toys with the possibility, an option, a dream, a potential that might yield something out of the tree.

Monolog relates also to the Zen koan of a tree branch falling in the forest which asks: "if no one is present does it make a sound?" Tal Gur

creates a silent monolog with the viewer. It is embedded in the form. It is understood from within the design and the dialog between its components. The tree has fallen down. If just the designer heard it and did not speak, did it make a sound? As the Zen masters would challenge, can you position the tree trunk differently and reveal another possibility?

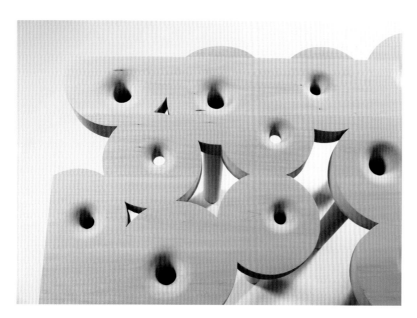

Redemption Table

NAME OF COMPANY | DESIGNER
Christopher Kurtz

SPECIFICATION
D1600mm × W736mm × H736mm

Redemption table is a continuation of Christopher Kurtz's exploration of the interior surfaces of wooden furniture. With its hollow legs, funnel-shaped cavities, and excavated voids, the table expresses the designer's sculptural intent. While computer driven manufacturing is increasingly the norm today, this one-of-a-kind piece is hand carved by Kurtz as a response to the increased desire for designers to be immersed in the creation of their work. The historic reference for this piece are the wood carvings of Tillman Riemenschneider and Grinling Gibbons; woodcarvers from the 15th and 17th centuries.

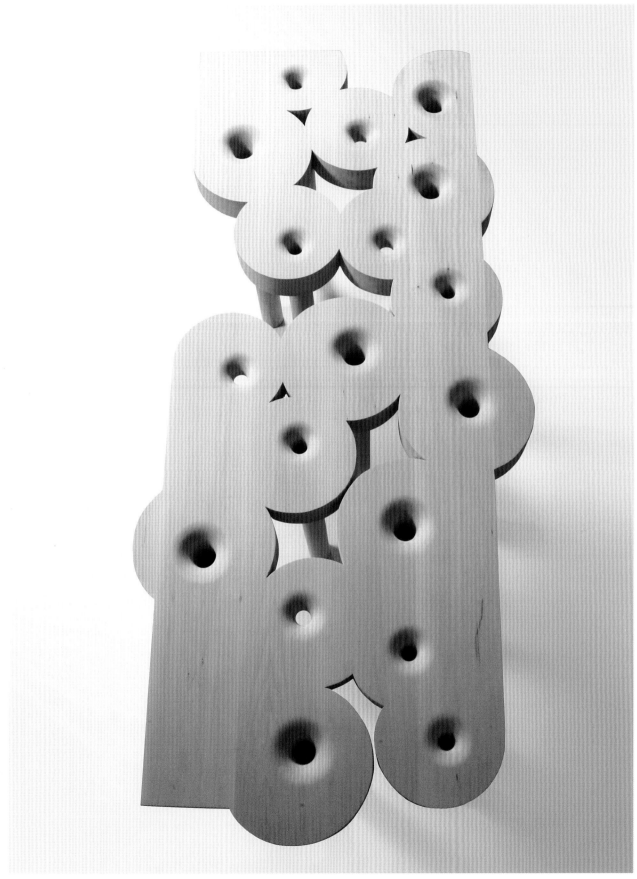

Joe Bear Central Bookshelf

NAME OF COMPANY | DESIGNER
Ibride | Benoît Convers

SPECIFICATION
L2060mm × W860mm × H1550mm

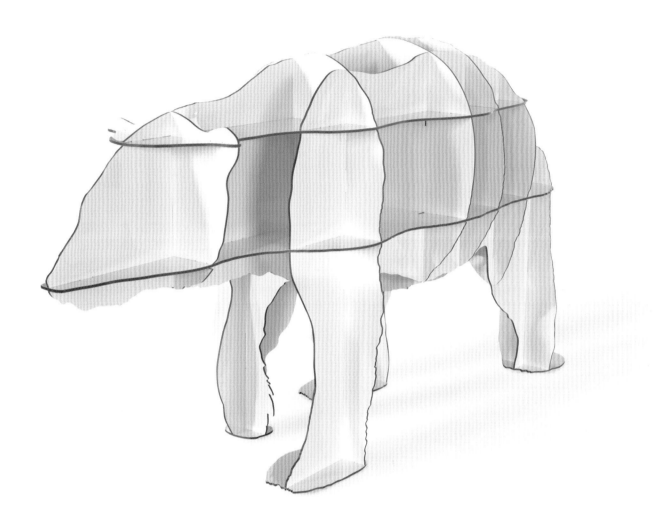

Junior Small Bear Central Bookshelf

NAME OF COMPANY | DESIGNER
Ibride | Benoît Convers

SPECIFICATION
L1800mm × W600mm × H950mm

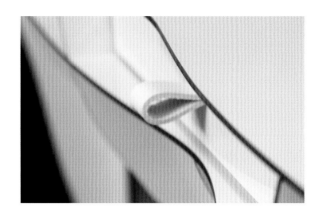

Elisee Pure Breed Console

NAME OF COMPANY | DESIGNER
Ibride | Benoît Convers

SPECIFICATION
L8300mm × W510mm × H1130mm

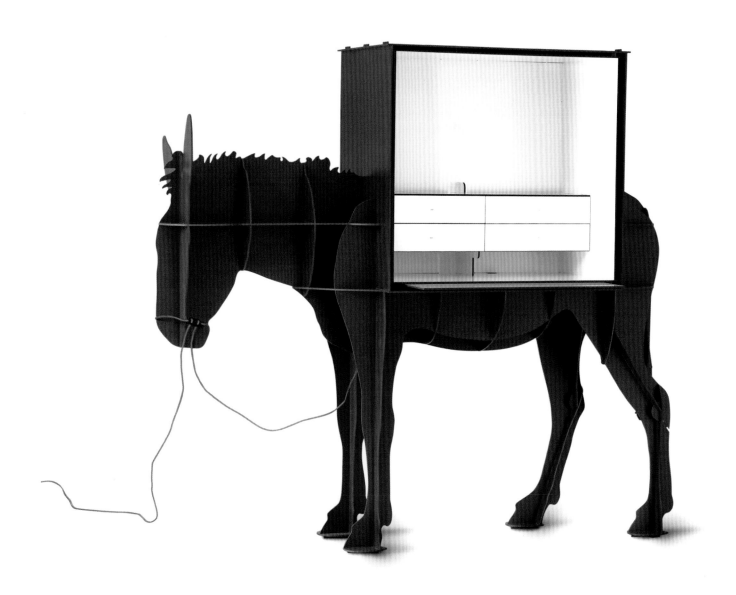

Martin Mule Wall Secretaire

NAME OF COMPANY | DESIGNER
Ibride | Benoît Convers

SPECIFICATION
L2000mm × W600mm × H1800mm

Diva Lucia Illuminated Ostrich Console

NAME OF COMPANY | DESIGNER
Ibride | Benoît Convers

SPECIFICATION
L1510mm × W920mm × H350mm

Diva Ostrich Wall Console

NAME OF COMPANY | DESIGNER
Ibride | Benoît Convers

SPECIFICATION
L710mm × W250mm × H760mm

Sultan / Zelda Dog Stool

NAME OF COMPANY | DESIGNER
Ibride | Benoît Convers

SPECIFICATION
Sultan: L520mm × W250mm × H340mm
Zelda: L620mm × W220mm × H260mm

Phone Bench

NAME OF COMPANY | DESIGNER
Elisa Strozyk

SPECIFICATION
L158mm × W100mm × H43mm

PHOTOGRAPHER
Sebastian Neeb

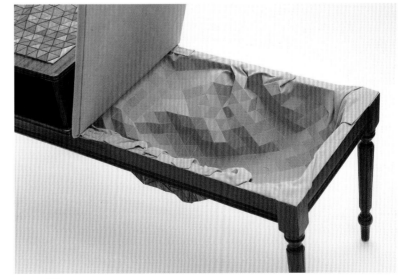

Accordion Cabinet

NAME OF COMPANY | DESIGNER
Elisa Strozyk

SPECIFICATION
H158mm × L100mm × W43mm

PHOTOGRAPHER
Sebastian Neeb

A collaboration with artist Sebastian Neeb.

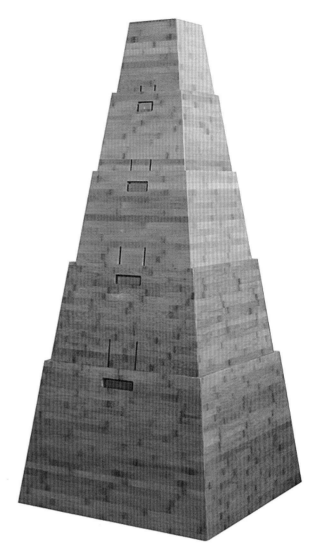

Bamboo Pyramid

NAME OF COMPANY | DESIGNER
Danny Kuo product design | Danny Kuo

SPECIFICATION
L550mm × W550mm × H1600mm

In collaboration with Soren Matz from MATZFORM/HHD, Danny Kuo designed the Bamboo Pyramid. The Bamboo Pyramid acts as a platform to showcase the qualities of bamboo for a travelling exhibition.

The installation is collapsible and therefore easy to transport during the exhibition. The piece also strives to show the qualities of bamboo, as both a material, and a plant. A bamboo plant is placed into the smallest box on top and will show its strength by surviving in unknown conditions and situations.

Double Desk

NAME OF COMPANY | DESIGNER
Danny Kuo product design | Danny Kuo

SPECIFICATION
H550mm × W550mm × L1600mm

Inspired by the keywords "efficiency," "maximum potential," and "lightness," the designer made this Double Desk. It primarily functions as a traditional desk, but for extra potential and efficiency you can pull up a secondary tabletop to either cover your primary tabletop, or extend your primary tabletop.

Staircase

NAME OF COMPANY | DESIGNER
Danny Kuo product design | Danny Kuo

SPECIFICATION
L550mm × W740mm × H2600mm

The most efficient way to build is vertically. Building vertically saves space as it uses minimal ground square meters. When it comes to interior design, the same rule can be applied. By focusing on height rather than width, efficient storage designs can be created. However, high storage designs can create a new problem because the higher storage parts will be difficult to reach. Staircase is a shelving unit that combines a bookshelf with a pullout stair system on the bottom three shelves. The shelving unit is 2.6 meters high and the top shelves are accessible by using the bottom shelves as steps for accessing the higher shelves.

33

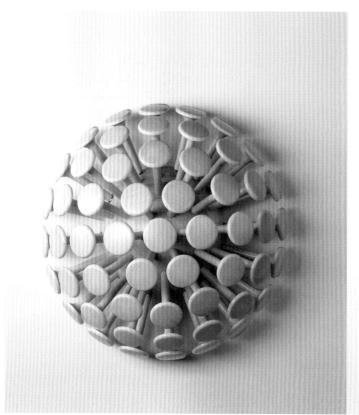
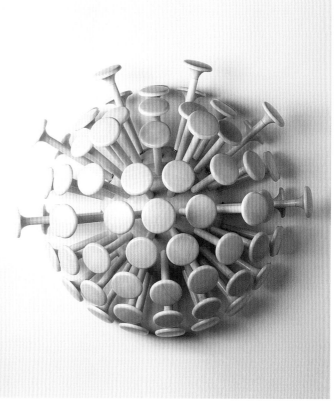

Dandelion Stool / Dandelion Coatrack

NAME OF COMPANY | DESIGNER
MOISSUE | Tsu Jung Kuo

SPECIFICATION
W450mm x D450mm x H425mm

PHOTOGRAPHER
MOISSUE | Li-Chieh Kao

Life needs more blossoms of light and imagination. MOISSUE seeks to challenge the limit of craft. After a primitive survey was done on the structure of the Taiwan woodwork industry, the designers decided to integrate traditional techniques and introduce the theory "Factory Big Volume – Finished Products Small Volume" to proceed with design. Dandelion subverts the stereotypical image of wooden furniture and serves a stunning visual feast – warm and strong.

"Life needs more blossoms of light and imagination." Designer Tsu Jung Kuo cleverly shows this design concept with the form of a dandelion. Dandelion is a piece of complex concept furniture. It can be a piece of art, a wooden stool, or even a magazine rack. In different spaces, it has different functions and tells a different life narration, depending on your imagination for life and space.

Dandelion provides a pleasant and warm atmosphere to any living space and MOISSUE hopes to awaken memories of the flavors of life by insisting on high quality production in design.

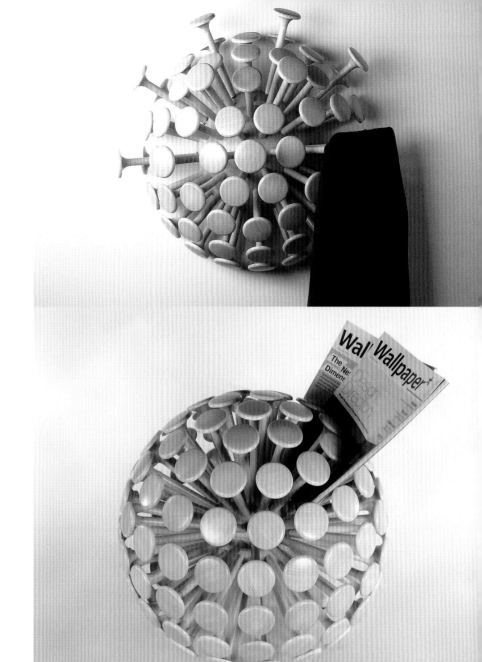

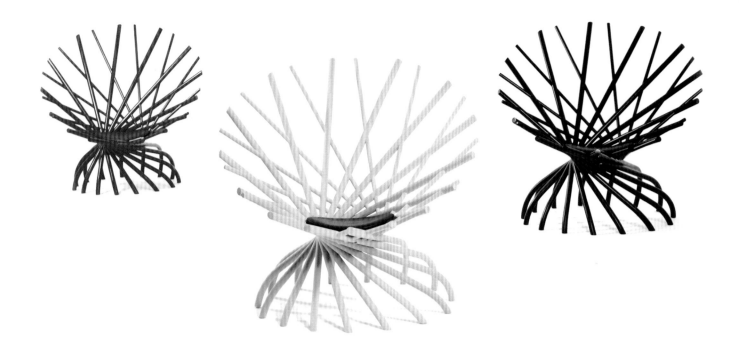

NEST

NAME OF COMPANY | DESIGNER
Markus Johansson

NEST is a piece created almost right out of the forest, which lets nature challenge the straight, rigid and traditional forms of modernist aesthetics. NEST offers a place in the home where one can relax and at a quick glance see a swirling chaos of pegs. The chair manages to offer a powerful illusion of movement and symmetry combined. The furniture is made out of a free form combination of round pegs without any "correct" angles, and is of course made entirely of wood. Markus Johansson has made use of both old and new technologies as the pins are bent and then drilled in a CNC-machine to achieve an exact fit. Each of the thicker pegs is identical and is cut at different lengths in order to alleviate production.

Markus claims, "design is about expressing a feeling that affects people and improves everyday life. I try to find inspiration in the strivings of mankind as well as in artifacts. My vision is to combine construction, function and form to enrich everyday experience. My goal is to create products with new shapes and lasting values."

NEST was first presented at Stockholm Design Week and has since been widely published.

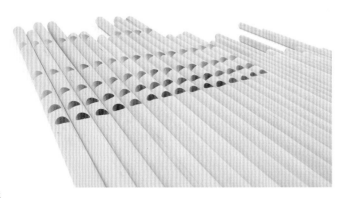

YELLY

NAME OF COMPANY | DESIGNER
Markus Johansson

This small and easy café chair is designed so parts can help one another to form a strong and visually exciting whole. The idea was to create a multi-purpose chair that is stackable, and also possible for coupling, that would fit into most homes and public spaces.

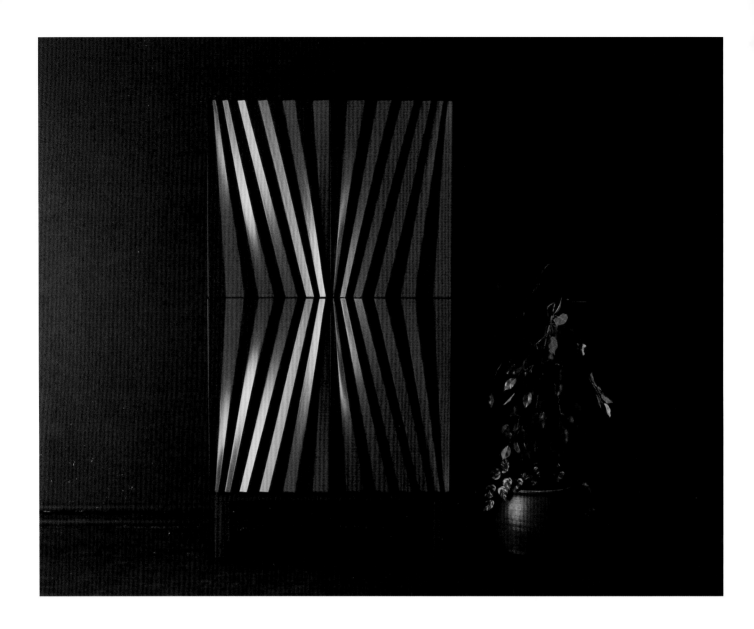

SAPPHIRE

NAME OF COMPANY | DESIGNER
Markus Johansson

SAPPHIRE offers a mesmerizing pattern that is both contemplative and playful. The character of Markus Johansson's exclusive cabinet is both tough and brave; and SAPPHIRE will thrive alone or with company, offering a reassuring and original centerpiece for both home and office.

SAPPHIRE is made out of two mirrored door halves that can be positioned freely in order to enhance different kinds of constellations. The cabinet is CNC-cut in MDF achieving an exact fit, while the undercarriage is made out of birch.

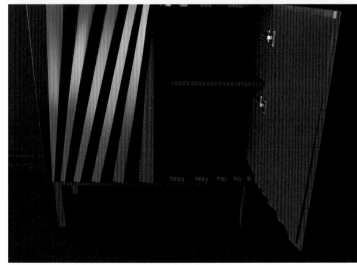

Tanz

NAME OF COMPANY | DESIGNER
ARTISAN | Grupa

PHOTOGRAPHER
Jasenko Rasol

By detaching the upper part with cutout handles, this coffee table instantly becomes a serving tray that both fortifies and holds together the construction of the table. Thanks to its negligible weight, it is very easy to move.

7

NAME OF COMPANY | DESIGNER
ARTISAN | Grupa

PHOTOGRAPHER
Jasenko Rasol

The basic features of this chair are the ergonomics
of its seat, legs in the form of the letter X and the
conjunction of elements that are not accentuated,
but merged into a whole.

Basic Collection: Basic Chair / Basic Armchair / Basic Table

NAME OF COMPANY | DESIGNER
ARTISAN | Grupa

PHOTOGRAPHER
Jasenko Rasol

Basic collection: the rustic warmth of wood was "cooled down" with minimalistic frames. The details have literally been carved into the corpus of elements, which at the same time both emphasizes and attenuates its solidity, depending on the needs and organization of the space.

43

Teascenery Deluxe

NAME OF COMPANY | DESIGNER
STUDIO MAKKINK & BEY

PHOTOGRAPHER
Rolant Dafis

Birdwatch Cabinet Girl

NAME OF COMPANY | DESIGNER
STUDIO MAKKINK & BEY

PHOTOGRAPHER
STUDIO MAKKINK & BEY

The birdwatch cabinet is a small sleep maisonnette for a young girl. A repurposed coat rack and a small chair create a separate reading cabinet space. By sandblasting the traveling box, the wood obtains a rich finishing.

Gardenhouse, bathstovetable and birdwatch cabinet are a series of products in which collected old pieces of furniture are combined, in search of new products and functions.

47

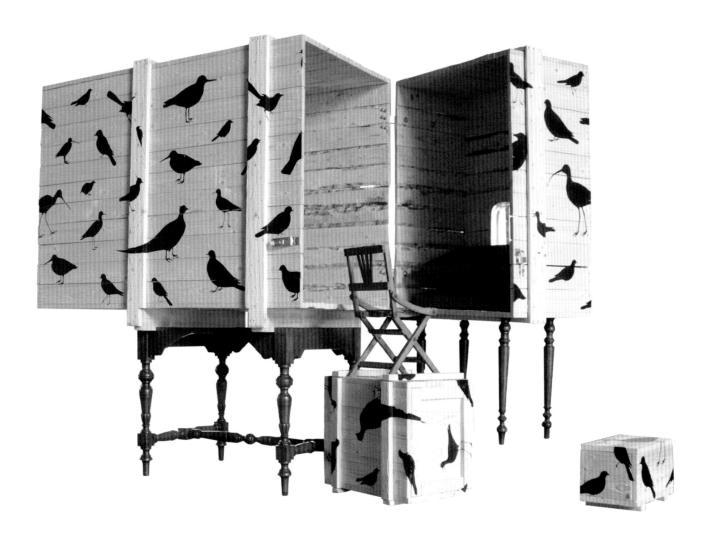

Birdwatch Cabinet Boy

NAME OF COMPANY | DESIGNER
STUDIO MAKKINK & BEY

PHOTOGRAPHER
STUDIO MAKKINK & BEY

The birdwatch cabinet is a sleep maisonnette for a young boy. An old table and office desk, together with a wooden traveling box, form a research-worker-cabinet. Once again the finish was sandblasted in order to create a rich finish.

Second Skin

NAME OF COMPANY | DESIGNER
designstudio Lotte van Laatum

SPECIFICATION
L800mm x W840mm x H650mm

The chair Second Skin is based on the cycle of wood. The wood from a tree is used for furniture, and for this design, this wood is brought back into its natural shape. Gathered branches have been 3D scanned and are translated into 3D milling work. Thus, the wood mimics its natural shape.

The wood is pieces of reclaimed oak furniture found at secondhand stores. The material is processed and takes on a new, high quality form. The shape of the chair is based on the shape of a tree, conical. The design of the upholstery references an overgrown structure in nature. The textile of the upholstery is made from 80% recycled materials.

Special thanks to Prins Bernhard Cultuurfonds.

Treecabinet

NAME OF COMPANY | DESIGNER
designstudio Lotte van Laatum

SPECIFICATION
L500mm x W200mm x H1300mm

The treecabinet is made of Dutch elm. The elm used for this cabinet was cut in 1999 as a result of the elm disease in Kloosterzande. The shape of the cabinet relates to the shape of the tree, conical and the same width as a large Dutch tree. The front of the drawer has been left untouched as a memory of the natural shape of the tree.

Felt & Gravity Sideboard

NAME OF COMPANY | DESIGNER
Amy Hunting

SPECIFICATION
H1000mm x W400mm x L1500mm

PHOTOGRAPHER
Carsten Aniksdal

Gravity is one of the components in this sideboard. The shelves, made from 100% wool, receive their strength from the weight placed inside them. The unit is created with a flat pack construction, and solid brass wing nuts and bolts keep it together.

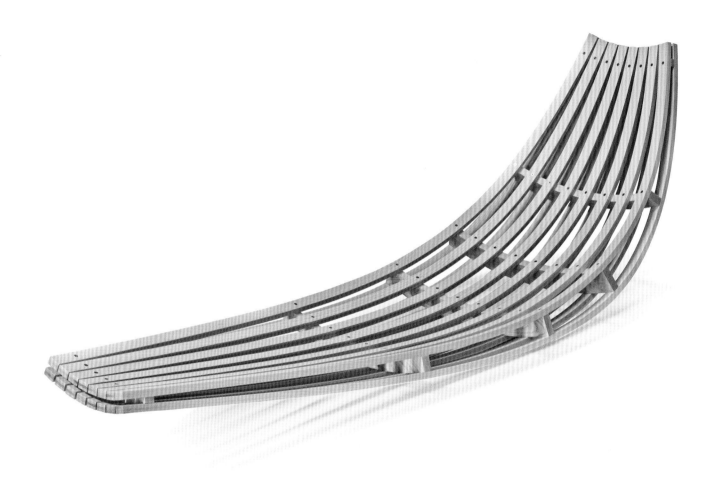

Glide

NAME OF COMPANY | DESIGNER
David Trubridge

SPECIFICATION
W600mm x L2200mm x H700mm

PHOTOGRAPHER
David Trubridge

This recliner, made of American Ash and stainless steel screws, is a Signature Design by New Zealand furniture designer David Trubridge. It was inspired by the casual and relaxed outdoor lifestyle of New Zealand.

3 Blocks

NAME OF COMPANY | DESIGNER
Kalon Studios

SPECIFICATION
H431.8mm × W431.8mm × D431.8mm

Designed to be one of those versatile pieces of furniture you can't live without, 3 Blocks is a set of 3 nesting tables or stools that play with the elemental shapes of the square, the circle and the line. The optional fern engraving is different on each of the 3 cubes. With lifelike precision the fern wraps around the edges, playfully overrunning the piece.

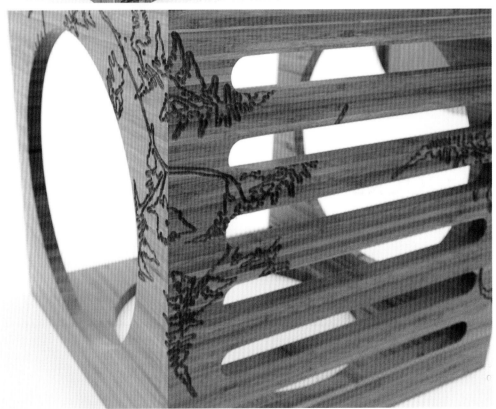

Stump by Kalon Studios

NAME OF COMPANY | DESIGNER
Kalon Studios

SPECIFICATION
Small: W215.9mm × H304.8mm × D215.9mm
Large: W304.8mm × H431.8mm × D304.8mm

Stump is inspired by the original sitting stool: a tree stump. Cut from the green wood of a tree trunk, the surface splits as it ages and dries, giving each piece a unique look. The raw and unfinished piece celebrates the natural qualities of the tree trunk. Stump explores the playful relationship between the inherent variations of natural materials and the precision of contemporary form. In these pieces, simple, contemporary form has been applied to a natural material that will break the form as it ages, making each piece unique.

Hut-Hut

NAME OF COMPANY | DESIGNER
Kalon Studios

SPECIFICATION
W698.5mm × H349.25mm × D698.5mm

Hut-Hut (Giddy-up for Camels) is a grown-up reinterpretation of the rocking horse. Made on a 5-axis CNC machine, the engraved star pattern is both a decorative element and an efficient use of machining time. Rather than resurfacing the piece to hide the machining lines, these lines have been incorporated into the piece as a decorative element, reducing the surface's machining time by 75%. Available in Bamboo, Black Locust, Black Walnut, Cork, and Maple. All FSC-Certified. There is also a version for kids.

Eyrie Chair

NAME OF COMPANY | DESIGNER
Studio Floris Wubben

PHOTOGRAPHER
Studio Floris Wubben

The nest of a bird is an inventive piece of natural architecture. The designer, who often works with natural material, was always fascinated by these structures found in nature. The Eyrie Chair is an ode to these natural constructions.

During the search for branches the designer was specifically interested in their forms. The specific forms of these wooden branches inspired the overall design aesthetic.

For the construction of the nest, steam-bended ash was used. The connections between the ash slats were made by an ash pin and wood glue. The frame was formed by wooden branches.

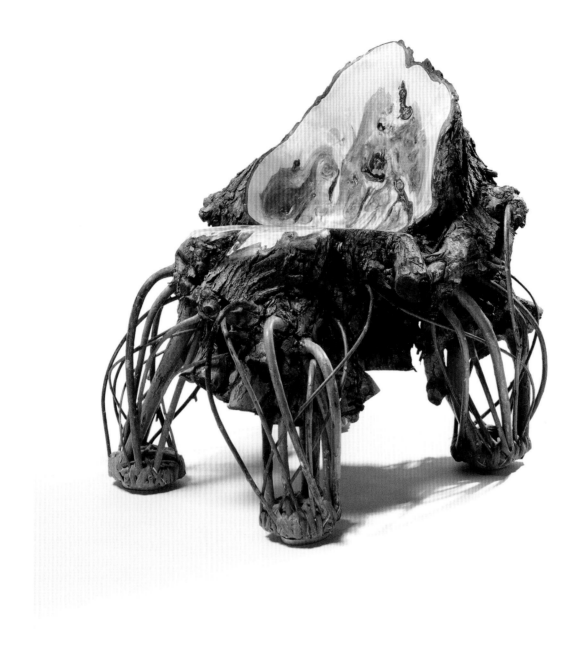

Upside Down

NAME OF COMPANY | DESIGNER
Studio Floris Wubben

PHOTOGRAPHER
Studio Floris Wubben

This chair is made from a willow tree. The configuration of the legs was obtained by twisting and splinting its branches. It was then allowed to dry into its final shape.

The seat and back were naturally kept in line with the bole's silhouette. This project was created jointly with Bauke Fokkema.

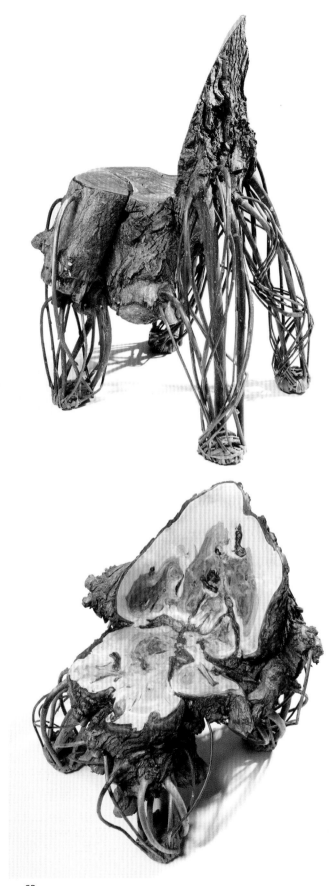

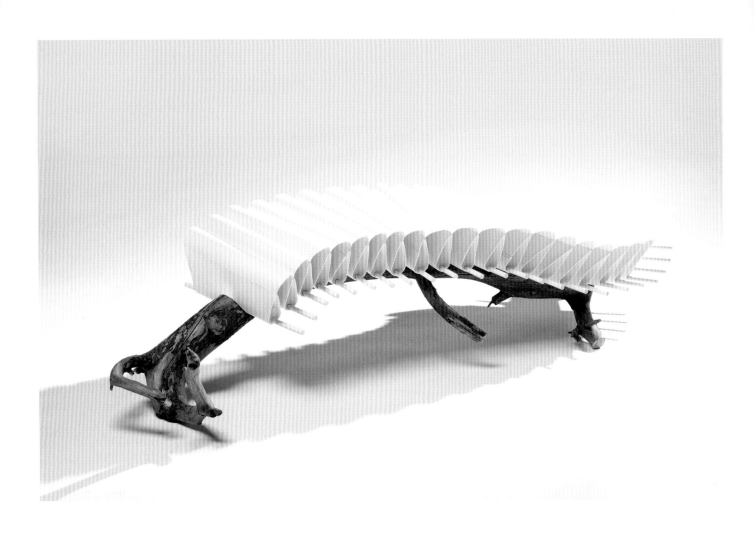

No.3 Bench

NAME OF COMPANY | DESIGNER
Studio Floris Wubben

PHOTOGRAPHER
Studio Floris Wubben

This bench is made of polypropylene, wood and lacquered metal. The wavy polypropylene is attached to the wooden branch with metal rods. As a consequence, the shape of the polypropylene is a similar shape of the branch.

The polypropylene forms a fascinating combination along with the natural wood. Although completely different, they both need each other to conquer the whole design.

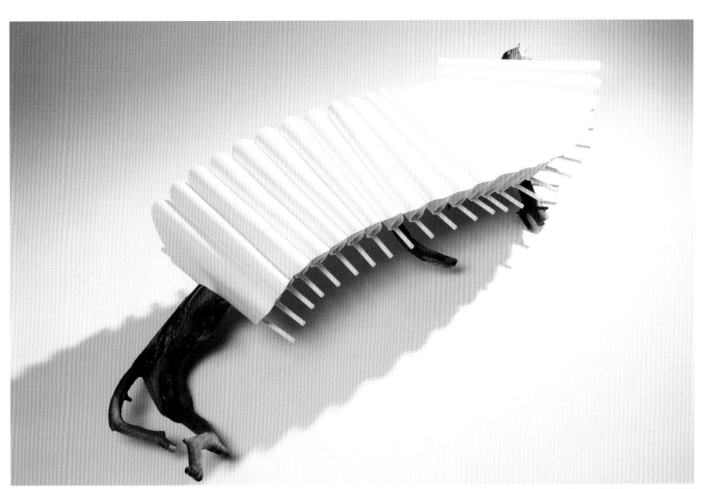

Tree Fungus

NAME OF COMPANY | DESIGNER
Studio Floris Wubben

PHOTOGRAPHER
Studio Floris Wubben

The design for Tree Fungus was inspired by two halves of a pollard willow tree; connecting the two halves is a parasite-like structure. Out of this construction a room divider arises.

When a willow stem is opened there is often fungi and mold, these organisms inspired the parasite-like structure.

The pollard willow is a typical Dutch tree, but construction projects have seen a decline of these trees in nature. The willow used in Tree Fungus was cut down for such a project.

This design project was put in practice with artist Bauke Fokkema.

Dominique – Coat Rack

NAME OF COMPANY | DESIGNER
StudioKahn and Sholi Strauss

SPECIFICATION
L500mm × W500mm × H1570mm

PHOTOGRAPHER
Oded Antman

The hard durability of the wood meets the fragile gentleness of the ceramic. This connection, combined with the different styles of the designers, creates a unique, new and exciting language.

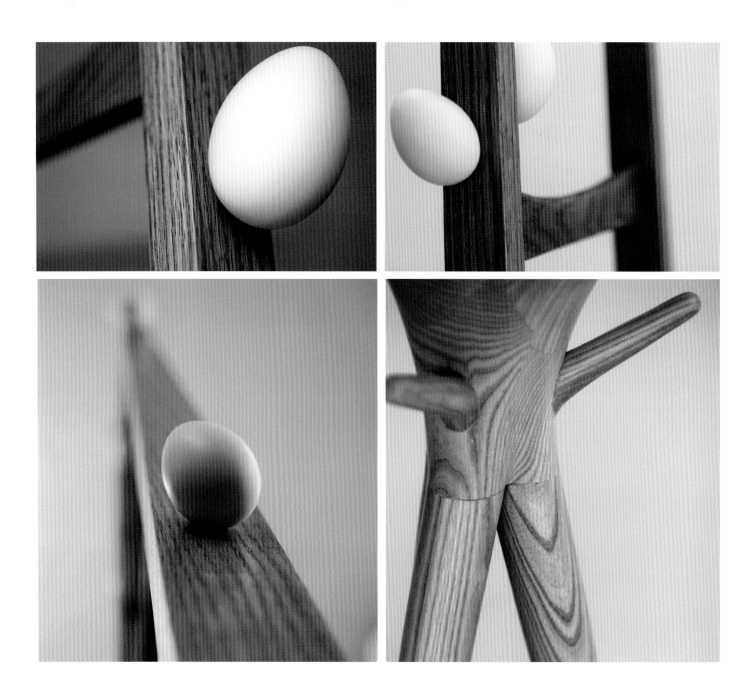

The Dream – Coat Hanger

NAME OF COMPANY | DESIGNER
StudioKahn and Sholi Strauss

SPECIFICATION
L800mm × W450mm × H2330mm

PHOTOGRAPHER
Oded Antman

This furniture, made for Sotheby's "Dream Object" exhibition, tells stories. The stories are not verbal; they are associative fragments, historic quotes from non-existing cultures passed on by unreliable witnesses.

3x3

NAME OF COMPANY | DESIGNER
3PATAS

SPECIFICATION
L1100mm x W400mm

3x3 is a collection of auxiliary tables, which neatly combine to form a family. After researching different users, the designers found that in many cases, they were living with limited space (such as inner city lofts) and were searching for solutions that could adapt to their various requirements. Whether it be entertaining friends, having a coffee, watching TV or simply having a dinner, the adaptability of 3x3 makes the table an attractive solution for these users. The large, main table contains two smaller tables, which users can remove and use independently. When the smaller tables are removed from the main one, two bowls fit perfectly in the spaces, modifying the functionality of the table. The bowls can be used to put fruit, children's toys or even be used as an ice bucket for drinks during a party. Users can define and create their own space by playing with different elements of 3x3.

The table's design allows it to be easily transported both during distribution or simply moving house. The table legs can be easily removed and the different elements boxed together.

The Wake

NAME OF COMPANY | DESIGNER
Studio ubico

SPECIFICATION
Basic Log: D350mm x H450mm
Log with Branch: D350mm x H400mm
Chair: D350mm x H480mm

PHOTOGRAPHER
Shahar Tamir

The "wake" is a collection of stumps, debating issues of material origin and lifecycle, natural material and technology, and the role of design as a mediator between consumption and criticism.
The series is handcrafted, and explores the limits of man-made objects that imitate nature—not a glorified nature, but rather, a nature tempered by man.
All the wood in the objects is 100% reclaimed and comes from everyday sources (dumpsters and scrap waste found in industrial areas, and the streets of Tel Aviv).
The series includes stools, a chair and a low table.

Stump

NAME OF COMPANY | DESIGNER
Studio ubico

SPECIFICATION
L300mm × W300mm × H400mm

PHOTOGRAPHER
Shahar Tamir

The primary aim in "stump" series was to generate objects that could be mass produced for a reasonable price, which visually enclosed their recycled nature in a sophisticated and desirable manner.

The process started in a study of potential raw materials and ended up focusing on relatively small pieces of hardwood thrown out in large quantities by the carpentry industry.

Studio ubico aimed (and hit) the "just under $200" price range, however, the main obstacle was the labor intensiveness of the design. This was addressed by passing parts of the production to a factory that operates a rehabilitation program for disabled people who are otherwise unemployed.

The potential for achieving the added value that was integrated into the work, and the production attempts undertaken at the factory, lead to changes in the design that enabled a better collaboration.

Simultaneously, specific aids were developed to support the people working on the "stump" series.

Legged Cabinet

NAME OF COMPANY | DESIGNER
Studio ubico

SPECIFICATION
L1160mm × W670mm

PHOTOGRAPHER
Shahar Tamir

This object started as a refitted, ready-made drawer, cut angularly at its back and fitted with two ready-made legs. This model was later refined and became a small magazine/book stand, made from reclaimed wood and ready-made legs. Later on, the object's proportions changed, enabling it to serve as a more functional cabinet. The process of shifting from ready-made based objects, to recycled material based objects, is a highly effective way to keep the visual content of the ready-made object, while pushing forward the object's function and role.

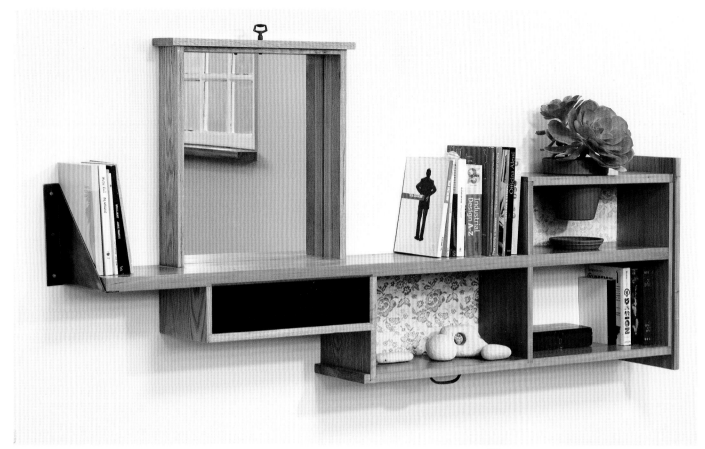

Salvadrawer

NAME OF COMPANY | DESIGNER
Studio ubico

SPECIFICATION
W180mm × H78mm × D21mm

PHOTOGRAPHER
Shahar Tamir

This piece offers a combination of functional and aesthetic quality that aims to spruce up the mundane book shelves.

The piece is the outcome of a study of thrown out drawers and raises questions regarding the context of the original drawer as a secretive and secluded space, in juxtaposition to the exposed new space and position the drawer has in this piece.

The 39cm × 42cm mirror and the terracotta pot plant combined with the decorative back, offer a different approach to books and artifacts showcased in living spaces and play on the role of objects as a new, though old, furniture piece.

Atlas Chair

NAME OF COMPANY | DESIGNER
Scott Jarvie

SPECIFICATION
L550mm x W750mm x H760mm

PHOTOGRAPHER
Scott Jarvie

The Atlas Project explores the possibilities of rationalizing complex surface geometries in a manner that resolves a number of challenges associated with translating sculptural computer generated forms into constructible fundamentals. The intention was to devise a principle that would be relevant beyond furniture, offering sculptural possibilities at a variety of scales. The thinking behind the project informed both the Atlas Chair and Jarvie's Fingerprint Pavilion, which was proposed for the grounds of the Lightbox Gallery in Woking, England.

The project was developed by experimenting with 3D computer generated forms and physical models. To encompass the strong visual ties with bone structures and the natural world, the project was named after the Atlas bone, which is the first cervical vertebra of the spine.
The Atlas Chair was derived by projecting flat angled planes through a volume and using the intersecting elements to generate the profiles that create the sections of the chair. This allows complex surface geometry to be rationalized to planar surfaces, allowing sculptural possibilities

while being material efficient and creating a system that facilitates construction.
NESTA invited Scott Jarvie to showcase the Atlas Project at their London Headquarters. The exhibition consists of the Atlas Chair and Table plus two sculptural pieces that underpin the thinking behind the project.

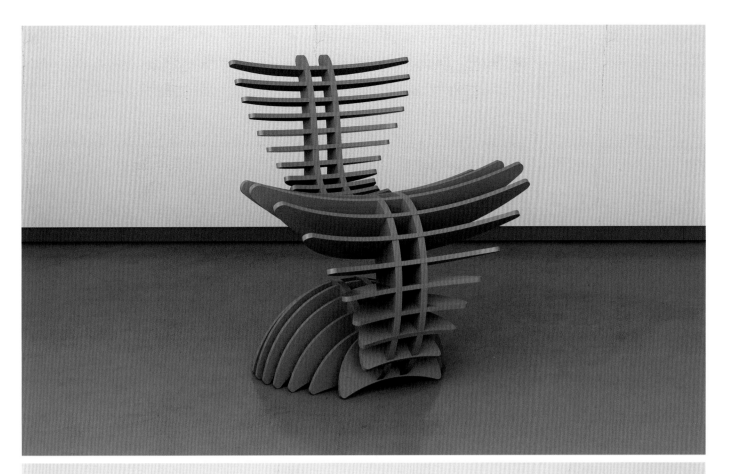

One Cut Chair

NAME OF COMPANY | DESIGNER
Scott Jarvie

SPECIFICATION
L480mm x W520mm x H740mm

PHOTOGRAPHER
Scott Jarvie

The One Cut Chair is water-jet-cut from a single sheet of plywood. A single continuous cut is made to produce the features that will form the seating surface and lumbar support when folded out. Thus the chair can be manufactured quickly and easily, eliminating the need for labor intensive and time consuming methods associated with traditional furniture construction. The design aims to make the most economical use of the material while minimising the energy required for manufacture.

Unlike a traditional slatted chair, where the slats are individually joined to the frame (which can result in more than 20 individual timber joints per chair), the One Cut Chair is laminated, resulting in the joining of only 3 or 5 timber elements, by means of lamination. The supporting frame is dip coated mild steel and provides a simple but effective means of support for the timber component. The design typology could also be applied to stacking chairs.

The design concept was developed by creating a series of 1:10 scale models in paper and card. This allowed aesthetic and ergonomic possibilities to be explored at a small scale, as, by small adjustments to the process, the chair can be subtly altered to offer a variety of appearances and seating positions.

Squash Me

NAME OF COMPANY | DESIGNER
Ross Gardam

SPECIFICATION
L785mm × W580mm × H790mm

Squash Me is a playful lounge chair that challenges conventional notions of seating support. The chair features curved slats that are individually cushioned by squash balls, making for an organic and direct response between body and object. The chair is constructed from plywood, steel and 13 squash balls.

Levity

NAME OF COMPANY | DESIGNER
Tervhivatal

SPECIFICATION
L1700mm × W500mm × H600mm

PHOTOGRAPHER
Tamás Bujnovszky

The young Hungarian designers of Tervhivatal made this prototype of a new recliner.
The chaise-lounge is composed of a 12mm thick birch plywood and 12mm thick birch rods.

Although the plywood shell is quite thin, there are twenty legs supporting it. The wooden rods are attached firmly in the drilled holes. This simple construction is lightweight and surprisingly sturdy.

Tree in the Meadow

NAME OF COMPANY | DESIGNER
Tervhivatal

SPECIFICATION
L2000mm × W400mm × H1700mm

PHOTOGRAPHER
Tamás Bujnovszky

The designers of Tervhivatal made this prototype from a new combination of a hanger and a bench. The composition implies a natural scene or a hayfield.
This coatrack and stool consists of 20mm x

20mm thick maple slats and an 18mm thick birch plywood. The slats are placed in a 50mm x 50mm matrix. Umbrella, newspaper, slippers, etc. can be stored among the slats. The top endings of the slats serve as a bench. The slats are placed densely

enough to create the sense of a continuous surface. This resulted in the experience of a strikingly comfortable sitting.

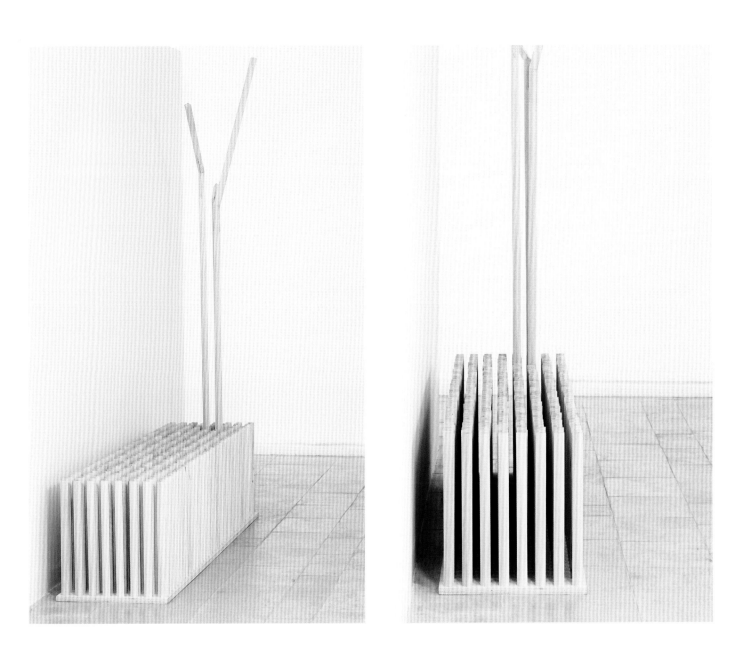

Ply High

NAME OF COMPANY | DESIGNER
Ross Gardam

SPECIFICATION
L1950mm × W850mm × H735mm

Ply High is a contemporary table which highlights the beauty of plywood. The legs of the product are cut from the underside of the tabletop to reduce material waste. As a variation to the natural appearance of ply, the tabletop is available in a number of laminate or linoleum finishes. This product is constructed from sustainably sourced plywood.

Flint

NAME OF COMPANY | DESIGNER
Ross Gardam

SPECIFICATION
Table: L2400mm × W924mm × H730mm
Bench: L2400mm × W428mm × H475mm

The Flint table and bench collection is available in an indoor and outdoor range. The leg detail was inspired from the principles of a lever and explores the idea of supporting the table using its own stabilizing weight. The tabletop is available in Australian spotted oak for outdoor use and horizontally laminated birch plywood for indoor use. The zinc plated steel legs are available in a full range of powder-coated colors.

Table

NAME OF COMPANY | DESIGNER
zizaoshe | Song Tao

SPECIFICATION
L1700mm × W750mm × H400mm

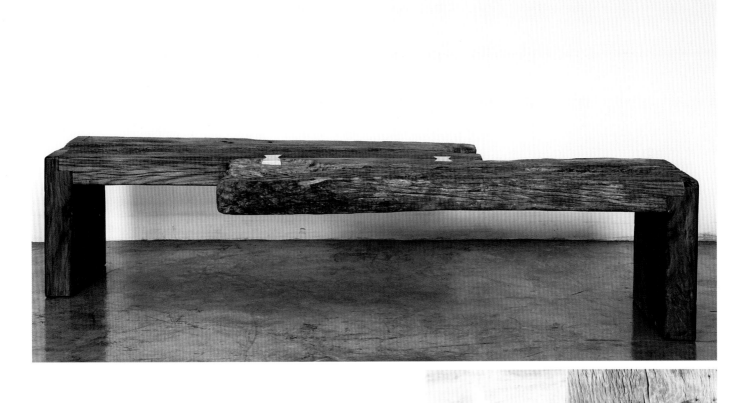

Coffee Table

NAME OF COMPANY | DESIGNER
zizaoshe | Song Tao

SPECIFICATION
L1700mm × W750mm × H400mm

Bamboo Coffee Table of Ming Style

NAME OF COMPANY | DESIGNER
zizaoshe | Song Tao

SPECIFICATION
L1600mm × W585mm × H400mm

Tome Chair

NAME OF COMPANY | DESIGNER
kaschkasch cologne

SPECIFICATION
D500mm × W590mm × H800mm, seat height 460mm

This is a chair with a high-quality crafted character. The soft transitions of TOME, especially its backrest, are a reminder of the characteristics found on plastic chairs. TOME however, combines aesthetics with seating comfort. The chair is inspired by Scandinavian design.

Pina Side Table

NAME OF COMPANY | DESIGNER
kaschkasch cologne

SPECIFICATION
Side Table Small: 420mm
Side Table Large: 500mm
Tabletop Round: 390mm
Tabletop Square: 380mm

Pina side table is characterized by its material and its certain appearance. Modern craftsmanship gives the side table its special character. The color stained surface adds what is needed for a young and fresh look.

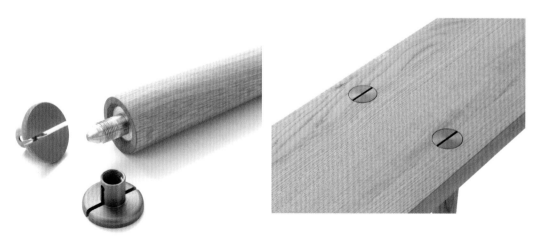

Høninger

NAME OF COMPANY | DESIGNER
kaschkasch cologne

SPECIFICATION
Table: L2000mm x H730mm x W680mm
Bench: L2000mm x H430mm x W30mm

This table-/bench-set is made of solid wood. The legs are fixed with anodized joints. This piece of furniture is inspired by Scandinavian design.

Armchair: D825mm × W675mm × H715mm
Side Table: D675mm × W675mm × H415mm

Wooden Comb

NAME OF COMPANY | DESIGNER
Duoxiang

This series of works is called "Wooden Comb." The wooden tooth becomes elastic through cutting. Due to different depths of cutting, they are different in elasticity. Hence, the elasticities in vertical and parallel directions to the wooden tooth are different.

When seated directly on top of one of the pieces, one tends to slightly rock back-and-forth, therefore the relationship between the furniture and the floor is no longer absolute. When people are transitioning from sitting to standing, their shapes on the furniture will shift, giving the feeling of different elasticity on the pieces. When the objects collide, a reverberation is made from the wood.

Overall, the furniture of Wooden Comb offers people a subtle sensory experience.

Table: L1800mm × W750mm × H750mm
Stool: L375mm × W375mm × H450mm
Chair: L450mm × W375mm × H800mm

Chair: L450mm × W375mm × H800mm

Firewood Bench Collection: Věra and Zdeňka

NAME OF COMPANY | DESIGNER
Klára Šumová

SPECIFICATION
Věra: 420mm x 220mm x 850mm
Zdeňka: 320mm x 420mm x 420mm

PHOTOGRAPHER
Petr Karšulín

This bench and side table are made from the firewood the Zdeňka family stocked about 40 years ago. However, it did not end up in the fire. Due to a lucky chance, it was conserved in the form of half-rounded logs until it became the perfect material for processing. The wood from Central Bohemia forests, birch, hornbeam and ash tree, are combined with the steel frame construction. The surface is finished with comaxit.

Plywood Conference Table

NAME OF COMPANY | DESIGNER
Libor Sošťák

PHOTOGRAPHER
Kristina Hrabětová, Michael Tomeš

Plywood Conference Table is made out of birch plywood. The upper desk is made of a special inlaid pattern.

Mingxin Series: Arhat Bed

NAME OF COMPANY | DESIGNER
THRU | Wu Wei

SPECIFICATION
L2045mm × W800mm × H680mm

Mingxin Series:
Cabinet

NAME OF COMPANY | DESIGNER
THRU | Wu Wei

SPECIFICATION
W900mm × D450mm × H1000mm

Mingxin Series: Chair

NAME OF COMPANY | DESIGNER
THRU | Wu Wei

SPECIFICATION
D900mm × W450mm × H1000mm

New Story Series: Children Chair

NAME OF COMPANY | DESIGNER
THRU | Wu Wei

SPECIFICATION
L330mm × W285mm × H300mm, seat height 570mm

Stadsbank

NAME OF COMPANY | DESIGNER
Jan Gunneweg

PHOTOGRAPHER
Hanna Kalverda

This bench is inspired by nature's beauty. The wood has been left in a nearly natural state and is juxtaposed with the concrete of the city.

Juweliersbalie

NAME OF COMPANY | DESIGNER
Jan Gunneweg

PHOTOGRAPHER
Erik Boschman

The Walnut wooden desk was designed and created for Luciënne Jesse Jewelry on Beethovenstraat in Amsterdam. The desk is inspired by the shape of a ring. The showcase is designed in the same style.

Aita

NAME OF COMPANY | DESIGNER
Artmotional | Elisa Honkanen

SPECIFICATION
L500-2500mm × W30mm × H1500mm

PHOTOGRAPHER
Elisa Honkanen

Aita is an extendable room divider/coat stand. The initial idea was to pay hommage to the classic countryside fences and bring their light into a modern interior. The movable structure of Aita allows endless amounts of different configurations and allows the possibility to cordon off areas within an open space without taking away from their openess. It also providest the chance to create free improvised openings and closings with its shape (for example with pets or children). Aita can also be used as an extandable coat stand that helps structure the entry area of a house. "Aita" is Finnish and translates to fence. The construction is based on a repetition of a triangular structure in solid timber and it is both easily extendable and stable.

Aina

NAME OF COMPANY | DESIGNER
Foundry | Elisa Honkanen

SPECIFICATION
Small: L360mm x W360mm x H320mm
Big: L720mm x W530mm x H380mm

PHOTOGRAPHER
Foundry

Aina is a set of nesting tables designed to create an illusion of simplicity with interlocking wooden bars. In this project, the designer studied the classic wood working joints and found that interlocking wooden bars were the most interesting part of the aesthetics of tables. The joint itself gives a classic touch for the table, and together with the plain wooden round bars it creates a sensation of simple geometry and playfulness. Interlocking joints also help to control that the impression of the structure remains light, even if it is made in a total of seven horizontal round bars with four vertical round bars (which create table legs). The word "Aina" is Finnish and means always, implying that the tables are to be used, not just merely admired. The tables are made of oak and/or walnut.

Purist

NAME OF COMPANY | DESIGNER
Elisa Honkanen

SPECIFICATION
L490mm x W450mm x H805mm

PHOTOGRAPHER
Elisa Honkanen

The designer has been a fan of Angelo Mangiarotti's Eccentrico table for a long time, and wanted to see if it was possible to make a chair with the same concept, using gravity joints to build the structure of the chair. The construction of the Purist chair is fixed with two screws (lateral wooden bars on the heigth of the backrest) and with a neoprene rope that forms the backrest. The plywood board that functions as a seat stays in its place thanks to the inclined holes on the board.

Form language recalls old Windsor chairs, although an extremely reduced version of its "ancestors" (hence Purist). Purist Chair was presented during Milan Design Week in April 2012 and won first prize in The Interieur Design Awards (object category) at Biennale Interieur 2012, Kortrijk.

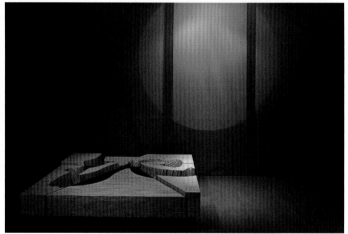

Ground Low Table

NAME OF COMPANY | DESIGNER
BANMOO | Lv Yongzhong

SPECIFICATION
L1800mm × W1500mm × H450mm

The thick beige plate is covered with cross grain, which appears as superimposed sedimentary layers of rock, with tracks left on the earth made by wheels. The hollowed-out cursive script, the Chinese character " 地 "(Ground), runs through the whole table, like the rushing Yellow River running across the Loess Plateau. It is running freely in mind, with body seemingly immobile.

Long Table

NAME OF COMPANY | DESIGNER
BANMOO | Lv Yongzhong

SPECIFICATION
L1850mm × W500mm × H885mm

This table is designed based on the traditional altar table in a hallway, with the modeling appearance absorbing the essence of Han Dynasty style, and the overall line of smoothness and elegance evoking the long sleeves of Hanfu in Han Dynasty. The table is made by the split joint of cutting solid wood. Brass fittings at the bottom of both legs highlight great ingenuity and extraordinary style.

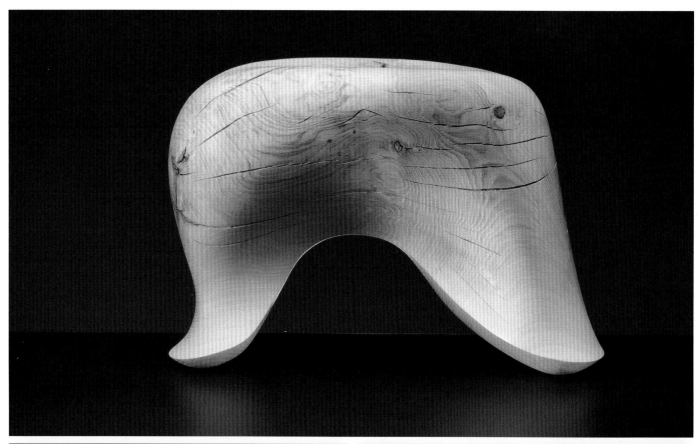

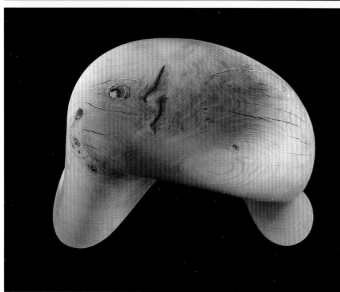
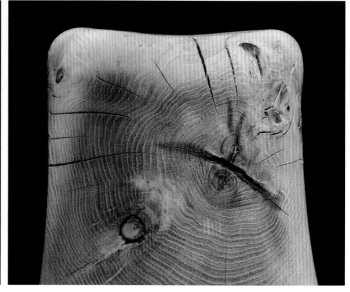

Tonus Stool

NAME OF COMPANY | DESIGNER
Rutger Graas

SPECIFICATION
L500mm x W350mm x H20mm

PHOTOGRAPHER
Erik and Petra Hesmerg

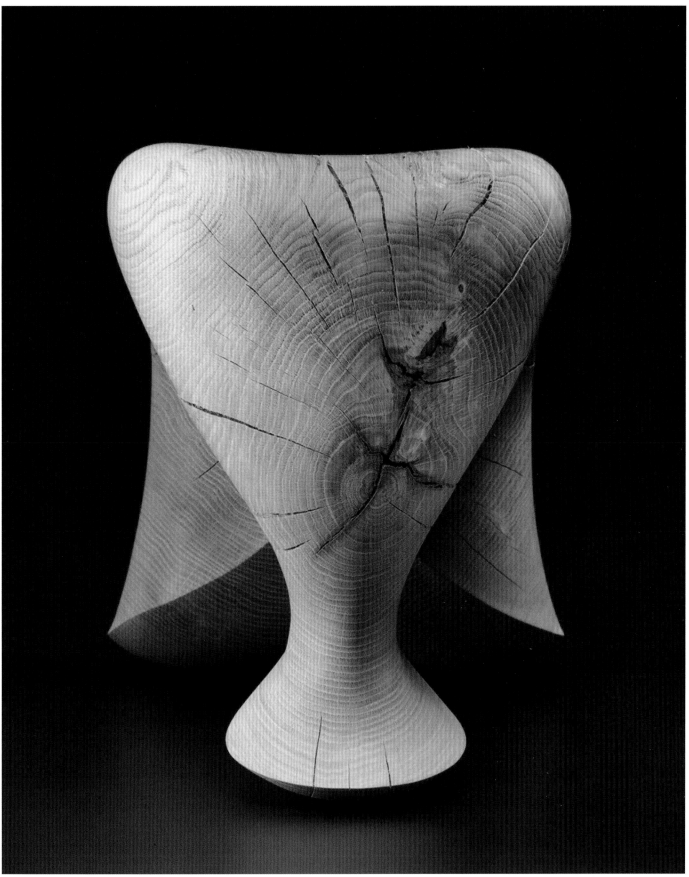

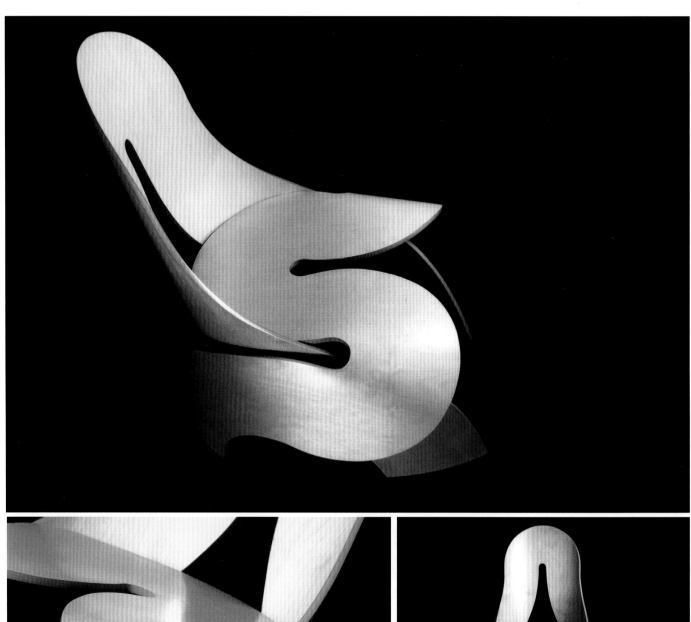

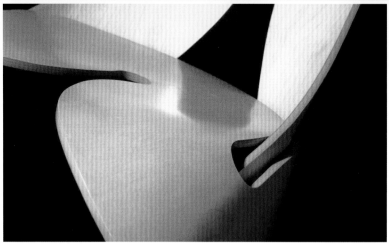

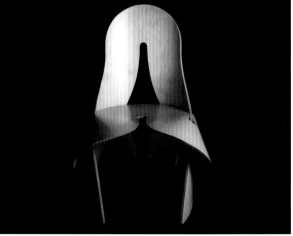

Fauteuil

NAME OF COMPANY | DESIGNER
Kevin Hughes and Aldo Bakker

SPECIFICATION
L730mm x W560mm x H520mm

PHOTOGRAPHER
Bas en Aldo

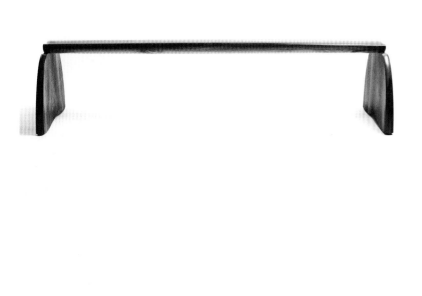

Pose

NAME OF COMPANY | DESIGNER
Rutger Graas

SPECIFICATION
L1900mm x W500mm x H450mm

PHOTOGRAPHER
Erik and Petra Hesmerg

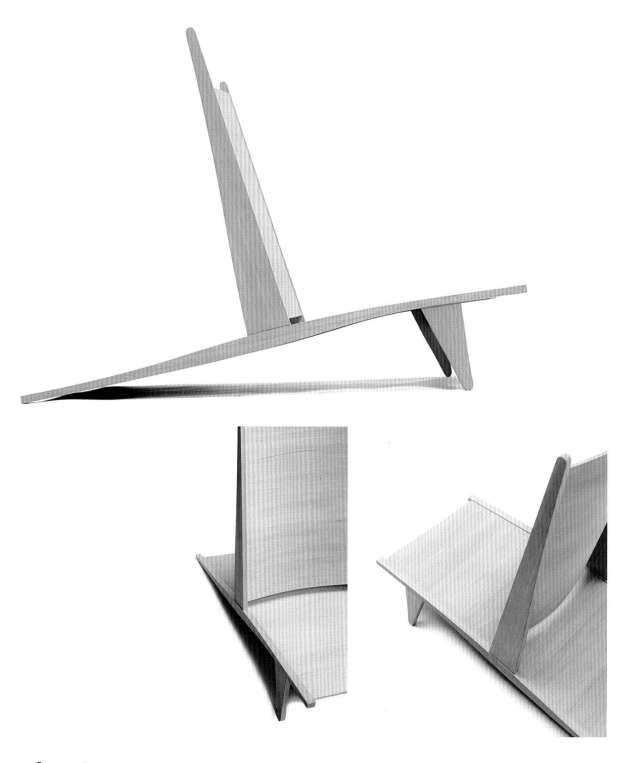

Low Chair

NAME OF COMPANY | DESIGNER
Aldo Bakker

SPECIFICATION
L1050mm x W750mm x H470mm

PHOTOGRAPHER
Wouter van den Brink

Float Bed

NAME OF COMPANY | DESIGNER
David Trubridge

SPECIFICATION
W3440mm x H2880mm

PHOTOGRAPHER
David Trubridge

This was a limited edition piece designed by David
Trubridge for Design Mobel.

Kissing Bench

NAME OF COMPANY | DESIGNER
Alison Crowther

SPECIFICATION
D450mm x W6000mm x H450mm

PHOTOGRAPHER
Swire Properties Ltd.

The design of Kissing Bench celebrates an old, romantic custom that allowed lovers to sit side by side, facing in opposite directions, yet were free to turn towards each other to kiss. Sourced from a single tree trunk, the bench is six meters long.

Its position in the lobby of Three Pacific Place, Hong Kong, China is aligned so that one side faces inwards towards the building and the other gazes outwards to the external world.

Mapping 2010

NAME OF COMPANY | DESIGNER
Alison Crowther

SPECIFICATION
D550mm x W1500mm x H550mm

PHOTOGRAPHER
Jacqui Hurst

Mapping was carved from a single piece of "Pippy" also known as English oak. "Pippy" refers to the clusters of tiny knots present in this rare type of oak, which are highly decorative. The oak tree originated from the woodlands within the Leconfield Estate in West Sussex, England.

The form of the sculpture was designed to accentuate the natural pattern of annual rings and thereby draw attention to the life and history of the original tree. The carved lines on this piece follow the annual rings as they navigate the form, the natural rhythms evoke memories of terraced landscapes, wind-swept dunes, or wave-washed ocean beds.

The original sculpture was procured for permanent display in the main lobby of a resort hotel near Guangzhou, China.

Twisting

NAME OF COMPANY | DESIGNER
Alison Crowther

SPECIFICATION
D900mm x W3000mm x H900mm

PHOTOGRAPHER
Heini Schneebeli

Twisting came about because Will and Kate Hobhouse wanted a long sculpture measuring some three meters. Crowther showed them photographs of the tree trunk she had sourced from the Leconfield Estate in West Sussex, and they considered this to be the perfect size. From then on Crowther was free to let the wood take her on the journey of making the sculpture. The form of spirals throughout the extent of the sculpture, carved with regard for incident and accident in the growth of the wood. The natural cracking emphasises the form, as does Crowther's carving, which follows the medullary rays along the length of the piece.

Ann Elliott August 2008 – from the exhibition catalogue of "Alison Crowther: The Ripple Effect," at One Canada Square, Canary Wharf, London.

Kidney II

NAME OF COMPANY | DESIGNER
Alison Crowther

SPECIFICATION
L1500mm x W900mm x H900mm

PHOTOGRAPHER
Heini Schneebeli

Sister piece to Kidney I, the carving here follows the annual rings around the form. The freedom of growth that this tree had in its lifetime is described with carved lines rippling out with the concentric annual rings from each center or "heart." It produces a texture reminiscent of worked landscapes or natural formations in sand, stone, and earth.

Shell III

NAME OF COMPANY | DESIGNER
Alison Crowther

SPECIFICATION
L650mm x W1800mm x H650mm

PHOTOGRAPHER
Heini Schneebeli

Shell III is the third piece of a tripartite sculpture, commissioned by a private collector in the UK. The forms begin to explore pushing beyond the outer layer or "shell."

Log Seat

NAME OF COMPANY | DESIGNER
Klára Šumová

SPECIFICATION
L1600mm x W1300mm x H700mm

PHOTOGRAPHER
Tomáš Souček

Felled tree trunks are commonly found neatly stacked near forest roads. The outcome is based on these piles and how they often attract a brief sit during a walk or hike. The goal was to create a functional piece of furniture by translating this common forest still life into a useful, pleasant and unusual outdoor element.
Log Seat is part of the "Settled landscapes" project and made out of pine wood and powdercoated steel.

Trunk Bench

NAME OF COMPANY | DESIGNER
Klára Šumová

SPECIFICATION
L1900mm x W440mm x H440mm

PHOTOGRAPHER
Petr Karšulín, Tomáš Souček

Reflected in this bench are the relationships between humans, nature, and the wood production processes. The wood is a borrowed material, processed at the sawmill to be returned, in some capacity, back to nature. Each board is assembled back into the original shape of the trunk; the manufacturing process itself becomes the bench.

Trunk Bench is part of the "Settled landscapes" project. It is made out of pine wood and powdercoated steel.

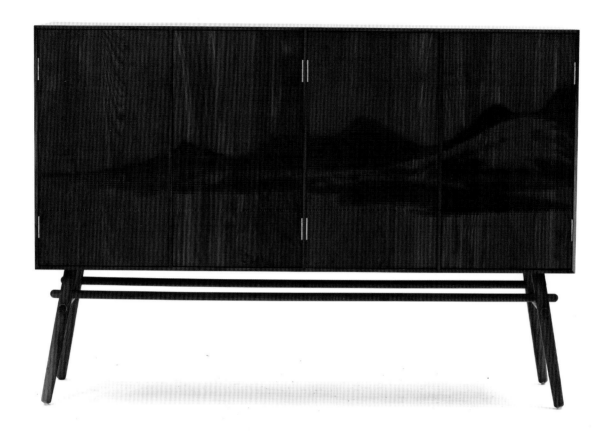

"Mountain" Sideboard

NAME OF COMPANY | DESIGNER
MORELESS

SPECIFICATION
W1600mm × D450mm × H1100mm

"Three Walkers"
Stool & Tea Table

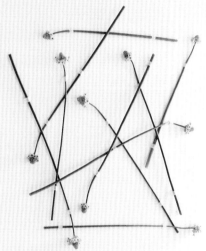

NAME OF COMPANY | DESIGNER
MORELESS

There is always someone to learn from. The organic furniture form comes from inflated spiral units. They bring about multiple functions and showcase the beauty of math.

SPECIFICATION
Stool: W482mm × D528mm × H549mm
Tea Table: W360mm × D328mm × H405mm

"Ignorance" Chair

NAME OF COMPANY | DESIGNER
MORELESS

SPECIFICATION
W580mm × D490mm × H890mm

This design pays homage to the Official's Hat
Chair of the Ming style.

"Arrange" Book Shelf

NAME OF COMPANY | DESIGNER
MORELESS

SPECIFICATION
W2030mm × D350mm × H2010mm

The robust form makes the changing patterns simple and clear. It is a depiction of The Eighteen Arhats, the original followers of Buddha in Mahayana Buddhism.

"Window Pattern" Dinning Chair

NAME OF COMPANY | DESIGNER
MORELESS

SPECIFICATION
W2030mm × D350mm × H2010mm

Diamond grain is a traditional pattern of window lattice, symbolizing a bumper grain harvest. It is an expectation for luck and happiness. By putting the design on the back of the chair it not only creates a clever visual effect, but also embodies good fortune.

Holzbank

NAME OF COMPANY | DESIGNER
Thomas Schnur

SPECIFICATION
W1650mm × D500mm x H900mm, seat height 450mm

Primarily found in forests and villages, conventional wooden benches are common in Germany. Crafted from untreated tree trunks, every one of them is handmade and unique. Inspired by the honesty and simplicity of this man-made object, this is a bench that, in terms of appearance, shape and materials, retains the fundamental qualities of the traditional wooden bench. An optimized, standardized processing technique reinterprets the wooden bench and gives it access to the urban environment.

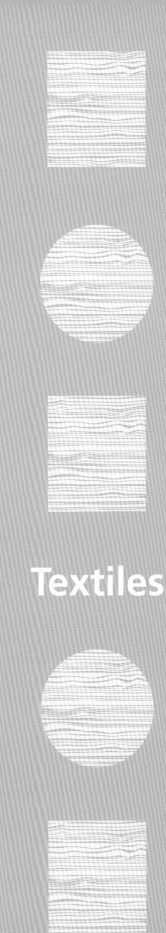

Textiles

Wooden Textile

NAME OF COMPANY | DESIGNER
Elisa Strozyk

SPECIFICATION
L1200mm × W2000mm × H0.6mm

PHOTOGRAPHER
Sebastian Neeb

A collaboration with artist Sebastian Neeb.

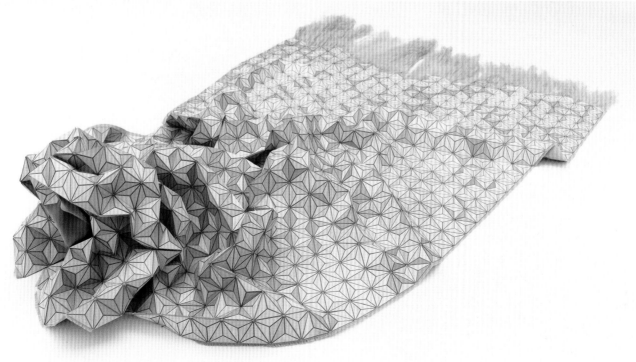

Wooden Rug: Grey Black Birch

NAME OF COMPANY | DESIGNER
Elisa Strozyk

SPECIFICATION
L1500mm x W2100mm

PHOTOGRAPHER
Sebastian Neeb

Wooden Rug: Mostly Red

NAME OF COMPANY | DESIGNER
Elisa Strozyk

SPECIFICATION
L1500mm x W2100mm

PHOTOGRAPHER
Sebastian Neeb

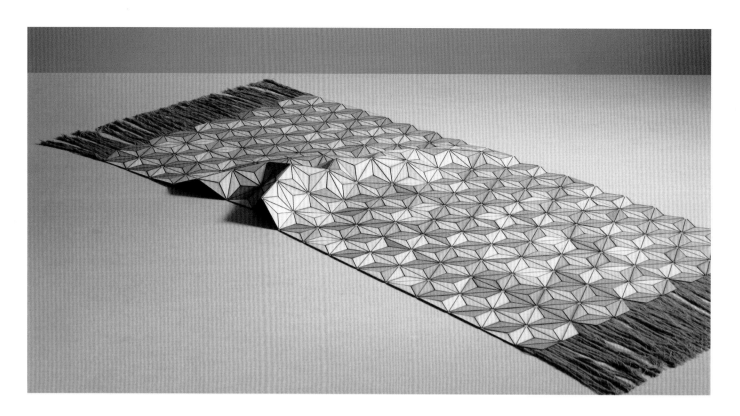

Wooden Carpet Ashdown

NAME OF COMPANY | DESIGNER
BOEWER | Elisa Strozyk

SPECIFICATION
L1520mm × W870mm

PHOTOGRAPHER
Axel Struwe

Lighting

Crimean Pinecone

NAME OF COMPANY | DESIGNER
Pavel Eekra

SPECIFICATION
L650mm x W650mm x H600mm

PHOTOGRAPHER
Alexander Nazaretsky

The Crimean Pinecone lamp consists of 56 plates and screws held without an internal frame. Light passes through gaps between the rounded forms of the plaques, which are slightly transparent themselves. This creates a special ambient pattern of light from the outside, while still exuding a practical downward-directed brightness. The lamp, which comes in a flat pack, has a natural wood veneer (beech), which further emphasizes the Crimean Pinecone's fusion of nature and technology.

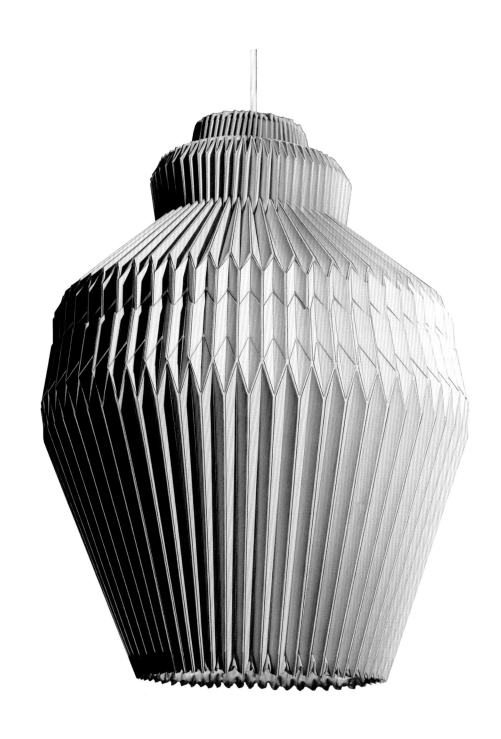

Accordion Lamp

NAME OF COMPANY | DESIGNER
Elisa Strozyk

SPECIFICATION
L350mm x W450mm x H450mm

PHOTOGRAPHER
Sebastian Neeb

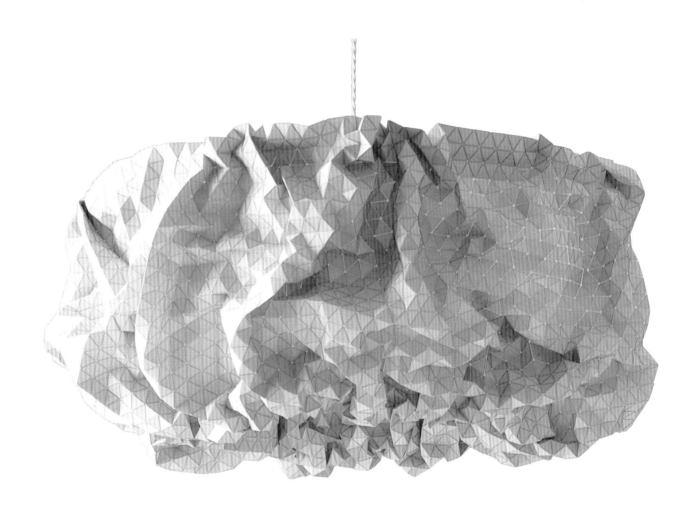

Miss Maple

NAME OF COMPANY | DESIGNER
Elisa Strozyk

SPECIFICATION
L850mm x W850mm x H350mm

PHOTOGRAPHER
Sebastian Neeb

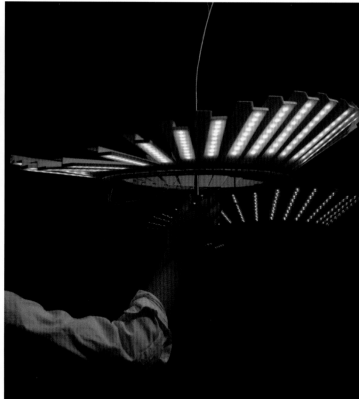

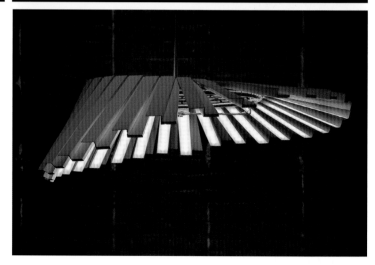

Liberty

NAME OF COMPANY | DESIGNER
Danny Kuo product design | Danny Kuo

SPECIFICATION
L650mm × W650mm × H500mm

Current developments in the lighting industry are changing the way lamps are designed: from the familiar light bulb to the fluorescent lamp, the LED to the OLED. Specifically the LED and OLED bring freedom, flexibility and adaptability for new lighting. To the designer, minimum size and the related flexibility are what inspire and interest most.

Designer Danny Kuo designed a lamp that is dynamic and functional in different situations. The lamp's light angle is able to adjust up to 180 degrees and the dimmer offers adjustability of the light intensity. These improvements in flexibility make the lamp adaptable for different contexts of a space where the lamp is used.

Flower Lamps

NAME OF COMPANY | DESIGNER
Laszlo Tompa

SPECIFICATION
L300mm x W300mm x H320mm

PHOTOGRAPHER
János Rátki

Designer Laszlo Tompa completed Cube Illusion, and decided to design hanging lamps. Similar to the cube, these lamps consist of wood turned elements. The basic geometric shape of the lamp is a hexagonal and pentagonal pyramid covered with geometric ornaments. The 'shade' is not transparent and light is emitted downward.

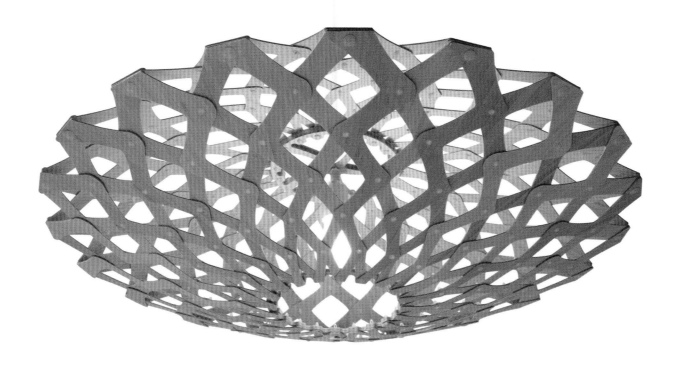

Flax Kitset

NAME OF COMPANY | DESIGNER
David Trubridge

SPECIFICATION
W800mm x H220mm

PHOTOGRAPHER
David Trubridge

The Seed System Kitset, comes flat packed and
is made from bamboo plywood and nylon clips.

Traces Shade

NAME OF COMPANY | DESIGNER
David Trubridge

SPECIFICATION
W270mm x H250mm

PHOTOGRAPHER
David Trubridge

Seed System Pendant Lightshade, made from bamboo plywood.

Stripped Concept

NAME OF COMPANY | DESIGNER
Studio Floris Wubben

PHOTOGRAPHER
Studio Floris Wubben

For the Stripped Concept design, a piece of nature is transformed into a standing lamp by a minimum number of modifications. It is an honest product, in which the natural form of the tree branch has been kept intact as much as possible. Stripped is made out of one only branch, which is split into three parts beneath. As a result, the legs of a standing lamp are made. The bark is almost entirely pealed from the branch, and with a rotating movement, formed into a lamp-shade. Each part of the tree branch obtains a new function, without losing its natural and exceptional appearance. The original form of the branch will determinate the final form of the lamp. Therefore, every lamp is a unique piece of design.

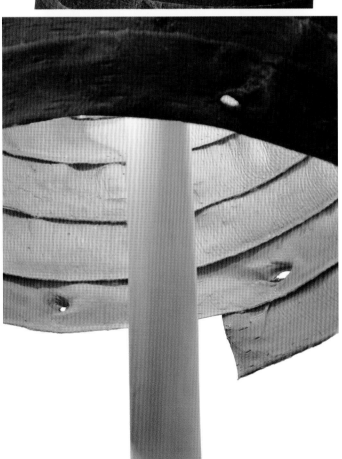

Oak

NAME OF COMPANY | DESIGNER
Ross Gardam

SPECIFICATION
D215mm x H260mm

Oak is a solid FSC timber pendant light. Each light shade is hand crafted and defined by the grain of the oak selected. The body of the light is accentuated by the intersecting hole, which allows a variety of hanging options with the cord wrapping through and around the hole detail. The light is available in one size and three finishes. Oak comes with a black shadow-line canopy to suit the hanging and a standard 2m of black cloth cable.

W2 Lamp

NAME OF COMPANY | DESIGNER
OOOMS | Pavel Eekra

SPECIFICATION
L600mm x W600mm x H600mm

PHOTOGRAPHER
Alexander Nazaretsky

W2 Lamp was inspired by the shape of radiolarians. Made of 12 parts connected by bolts and wing nuts, the parts are made of plywood veneer on one side. There are 6 ways to build the light, resulting in various forms.

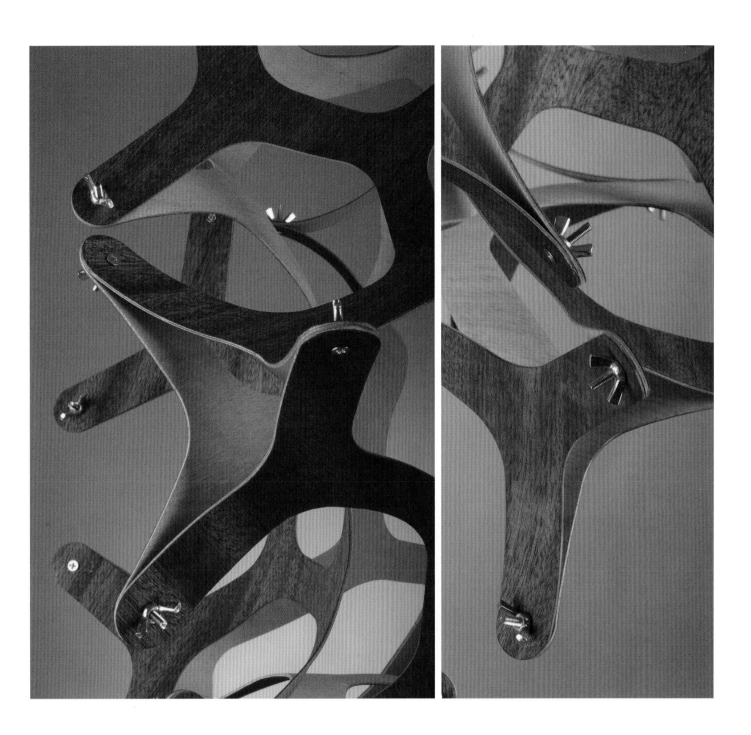

Creative Products

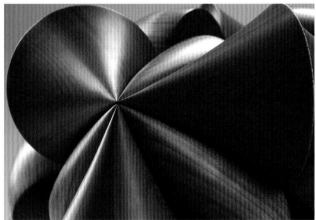

Cube Illusion

NAME OF COMPANY | DESIGNER
Laszlo Tompa

SPECIFICATION
L400mm x W400mm x H400mm

PHOTOGRAPHER
János Rátki

Not simply a wooden storage box with a lid, a cube is seamlessly covered with three different bodies of revolution that engage in each other, thereby producing a powerful geometrical design sculpture. The decorating elements create an optical illusion – one would not think at first sight that the piece contains a relatively large storage space. "Cube Illusion" was selected as an IFDA Asahikawa 2011 finalist.

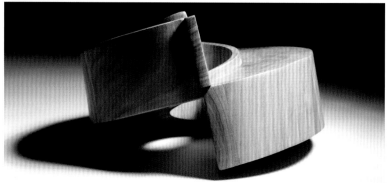

Spiral Box

NAME OF COMPANY | DESIGNER
Laszlo Tompa

SPECIFICATION
L220mm x W220mm x H130mm

PHOTOGRAPHER
János Rátki

This spiral-shaped wooden box contains a drawer. At first sight, it seems impossible to pull out the drawer from the box; however, the spiral shape enables it to be rotated fully onto the top of the box.

Spatula

NAME OF COMPANY | DESIGNER
Danny Kuo product design | Danny Kuo

SPECIFICATION
L300mm × W90mm × H7mm

The theme was "safety in the kitchen." After a wide-ranging research of kitchen hazards, the designer chose one that puts the food, rather than the person cooking, in danger. After cooking vegetables, noodles or pasta in hot water, a lot of people try to use their tableware or spatula to hold back the content of their pan in attempting to lose the water. Often you are just barely balancing between losing your water successfully and losing some of, or all of, your food in the sink. By creating this product, the designer combined the strainer with a spatula.

Dutch Wood

NAME OF COMPANY | DESIGNER
designstudio Lotte van Laatum

SPECIFICATION
div; appr 300mm x 400mm x 24mm

The cutting boards create awareness about the sustainable use of local resources. The shape of each board is based on the geographical shape of the region in The Netherlands in which the tree grew. The tree is cut by the Dutch Forestry Council (staatsbosbeheer) and is only harvested when it is necessary for the well being of the entire forest.

There are three different shapes of cutting boards:the Veluwe, the Noordoostpolder and the Sallandare, the names of the regions where the wood was retrieved. They are made of three different types of wood – beech, ash and maple.

Alder Bowls Stained with Iron on Oak Ground
180mm × 100mm

Handmade Spoons,
Bowls and Tableware

NAME OF COMPANY | DESIGNER
Nic Webb

PHOTOGRAPHER
Tif Hunter, Michael Harvey and Nic Webb

These spoons and bowls have been hand carved using traditional tools and techniques. The timber is worked green, (fresh living wood) and is collected on walks around the British Isles or overseas.

"When I begin carving I look for the differing qualities in each piece, allowing the grain and character to influence the design. Each spoon evolves to have its own personality and when finished becomes a showcase of the limitless beauty of wood."

Collection of Spoons in Various Woods
600mm

Brith Spoons
Indian Bean
Buddliea
Buddliea
Ash
Beech
Sycamore
Cherry
120mm

Lime Bowl
600mm × 300mm

Walnut Server
600mm

Salt and Pepper Spoons Holly and Cherry
55mm

Indian Bean Servers
300mm

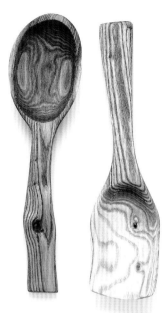

Group of Spoons
Walnut
Cherry
Silver Birch
Ash
Cherry
Willow
Willow

DOLCI

NAME OF COMPANY | DESIGNER
MOISSUE | Li-Chieh Kao

SPECIFICATION
FREE SIZE

PHOTOGRAPHER
MOISSUE | Li-Chieh Kao

When meticulous wood craft meets refined stainless steel, a lively carnival event begins quietly on the ears!

Under the unique refinement of "Anti-deconstruction Method," the "DOLCI" have distinct layers, just like dessert. "DOLCI" have both good taste and detail.

Every single "DOLCI" is supervised by MOISSUE himself for the final surface treatment. The natural vegetable oil wax makes the color of the surface moist, and also makes the expression of each earring rich, natural, warm and full of vitality.

Second Life Wood Ring

NAME OF COMPANY | DESIGNER
MOISSUE | Li-Chieh Kao, Tsu Jung Kuo

PHOTOGRAPHER
MOISSUE | Li-Chieh Kao

"Second Life" refers to the new purpose of the wood used in creating these rings. The pieces of wood used for Second Life came from the floor scraps of a wood factory. They were re-shaped, polished with a veneer and given a new, second life.

Date

NAME OF COMPANY | DESIGNER
WEWOOD

Stylish and sustainable, WEWOOD creates eco-luxury designs inspired by nature. They are a new way to be fashionable and close to Mother Nature at the same time.
WEWOOD crafts timepieces from 100% natural wood and plants one tree for every watch sold.

SPECIFICATION
L22mm x W11mm x H12mm

The main aesthetic ideology of WEWOOD starts with the use of ecological and not-toxic materials, then researching the ethical consumer, paying attention to environmental sustainability, and finally combining attentiveness for new trends and designs. For this reason, watch models are unisex,

PHOTOGRAPHER
Damiano Verdiani

which allows the largest number of people to be involved in the project of sustainability.
WEWOOD tries to reconnect people and nature. In this way, every owner of a WEWOOD watch will know they have made a small contribution against deforestation.

Jupiter

NAME OF COMPANY | DESIGNER
WEWOOD

SPECIFICATION
L20mm x W47mm x H13mm

PHOTOGRAPHER
Damiano Verdiani

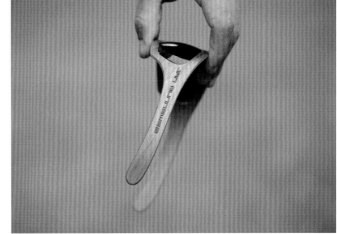

Houten Zonnebril

NAME OF COMPANY | DESIGNER
Jan Gunneweg

PHOTOGRAPHER
Jeroen Nieuwhuis

These wooden sunglasses wrap around the wearers face, providing a natural barrier to sunlight.

Bird Brooch

NAME OF COMPANY | DESIGNER
Scoops Design | Sophie Cooper

SPECIFICATION
D4mm × W40mm × H50mm

PHOTOGRAPHER
Sophie Cooper

A series of seven bird brooches: Puffin, Robin, Parrot, Finch, Parakeet, Toucan and Love Bird. Each brooch is laser cut from recycled plywood and hand painted. These brooches form part of Scoops Design jewellery range and are sold in boutiques and galleries around Australia.

Santa and Love Heart Christmas Decorations

NAME OF COMPANY | DESIGNER
Scoops Design | Sophie Cooper

SPECIFICATION
Santa: D4mm × W86mm × H77mm
Love Heart: D4mm × W80mm × H80mm

PHOTOGRAPHER
Sophie Cooper

Laser cut Christmas decorations are made from recycled plywood. The decorations form part of Scoops Design Christmas range.

Flower Brooch

NAME OF COMPANY | DESIGNER
Scoops Design | Sophie Cooper

SPECIFICATION
Various 4mm deep

PHOTOGRAPHER
Sophie Cooper

These brooches were commissioned for the Rupert Bunny Exhibition Shop at the National Gallery of Victoria, Australia in 2010. They were inspired by Rupert Bunny's Impressionist paintings of flowers. Each brooch is laser cut and then hand painted.

Mr. and Mrs. Fox

NAME OF COMPANY | DESIGNER
Scoops Design | Sophie Cooper

SPECIFICATION
Mr. Fox: D4mm × W280mm × H260mm
Mrs. Fox: D4mm × W180mm × H170mm

PHOTOGRAPHER
Sophie Cooper

Mr. and Mrs. Fox were designed for an exhibition in Sydney, Australia called Art By Design. They are made from laser cut recycled plywood and hand painted.

Owl Family

NAME OF COMPANY | DESIGNER
Scoops Design | Sophie Cooper

SPECIFICATION
Mr. Owl: D4mm × W280mm × H290mm
Mrs. Owl: D4mm × W180mm × H190mm
Baby Owl: D4mm × W105mm × H110mm

PHOTOGRAPHER
Sophie Cooper

The Owl Family were designed for an exhibition in Sydney, Australia called Art By Design. They are made from laser cut recycled plywood and hand painted.

Penguin Family

NAME OF COMPANY | DESIGNER
Scoops Design | Sophie Cooper

SPECIFICATION
Mr. Penguin: D4mm × W285mm × H300mm
Mrs. Penguin: D4mm × W185mm × H180mm
Baby Penguin: D4mm × W11mm × H11mm

PHOTOGRAPHER
Sophie Cooper

The Penguin Family were designed for an exhibition in Sydney, Australia called Art By Design. They are made from laser cut recycled plywood and hand painted.

Zoo Mobile

NAME OF COMPANY | DESIGNER
Scoops Design | Sophie Cooper

SPECIFICATION
(Various) D4mm × W160mm × H100mm

PHOTOGRAPHER
Sophie Cooper

The Zoo Mobile forms part of Scoops Design mobile range. There are four animals included: elephant, monkey, tiger and hippopotamus. Each set is made from recycled plywood.

The Dog, The Rabbit, The Hippo, The Monkey, The Rocking Horse, The Bear, The Elephant, The Royal Gaurdsman

NAME OF COMPANY | DESIGNER
Kay Bojesen Denmark

The Songbird

NAME OF COMPANY | DESIGNER
Kay Bojesen Denmark

The Bojesen's patio at the family home Bella Vista near Bellevue, north of Copenhagen, was full of flowers, wicker furniture and birds. There can be no doubt this was the source of Kay Bojesen's inspiration for the carefree songbird that he designed in the 1950s and hand-painted in cheerful colors. Even with the naked eye, it is clear that Ruth, Pop, Otto, Kay, Peter and Sunshine belong to the Bojesen animal family. All six birds have a clean, modern expression, stripped of superfluous details. And though clearly not an attempt to imitate nature, the birds are still so lifelike that it is easy to imagine they break out in song as the sun rises over the sound.

Hopper Boxes

NAME OF COMPANY | DESIGNER
kaschkasch cologne

SPECIFICATION
Small: 30mm
Medium: 50mm
Large: 90mm

Hopper boxes are an accessory series of boxes consisting of stacked cylinders in different heights. The gently projecting cylinders are a considered, functional and aesthetic aspect. The project is inspired by the traditional Japanese wappa bowl.

Trunks

NAME OF COMPANY | DESIGNER
Vyrobeno Lesem | Lenka Damová

PHOTOGRAPHER
Tomáš Brabec

This collection of jewel cases, with a mirror fixed to the top, evokes a group of cut down trees, a reaction to the rapid retreat of the forest. It holds the mirror of today up to us, pointing out the direction we are taking.

New Story Series: Candlestick

NAME OF COMPANY | DESIGNER
THRU | Wu Wei

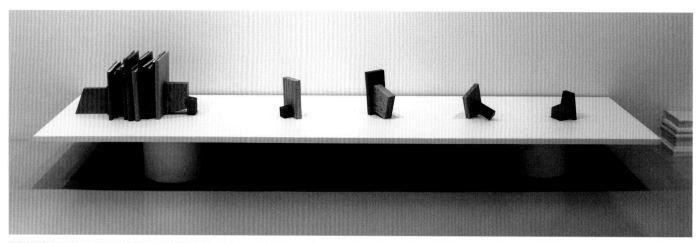

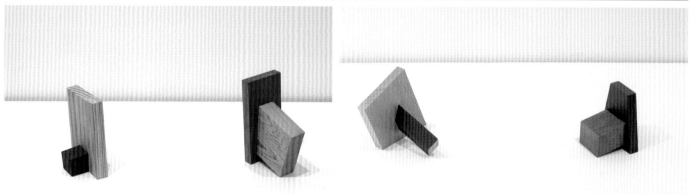

Book Ends

NAME OF COMPANY | DESIGNER
Amy Hunting

PHOTOGRAPHER
Amy Hunting

These book supports are made with different structures and shades of blue.
After the Felt & Gravity Collection, odd shapes of wood were left over, together with blue pigment from the Anamorphoscope. The two leftover materials were a perfect match and these book ends were created.

Human Bike

NAME OF COMPANY | DESIGNER
Jan Gunneweg

PHOTOGRAPHER
Jeroen Nieuwhuis

The inspiration for this walnut bike is based on man.
Two wooden spokes symbolize the two legs of man and create a striking effect during use.

The Human Bike weighs 15 kilos. The wood used in this handmade bike absorbs the vibrations during cycling, which results in an ultimate relaxing cycling experience.

Wooden USB Stick

NAME OF COMPANY | DESIGNER
OOOMS | Guido Ooms & Karin van Lieshout

PHOTOGRAPHER
OOOMS

USB sticks are always nice to have around when transferring files from computer to computer. The Wooden USB Stick from OOOMS is made to stand out from its natural environment of computers and offices. The sticks are picked from the woods and are individually selected for their natural beauty and then professionally handmade into unique and personal wooden USB sticks.

Puzzleboard

NAME OF COMPANY | DESIGNER
OOOMS | Guido Ooms & Karin van Lieshout

SPECIFICATION
L290mm x W175mm x H17mm

The Puzzleboard by OOOMS can be used in more ways than one. Each board can be used on its own as a cutting board or serving plate, or put some boards together and you have a super-sized your workspace. It is ideal for cutting those long baguettes. But the best aspect, is that any wineglass can be fitted into the open spot of a board. Using the boards at parties allows guests to enjoy both wine & delicacies, while still having one hand free to greet other friends.

Solar Birdhouse

NAME OF COMPANY | DESIGNER
OOOMS | Guido Ooms & Karin van Lieshout

SPECIFICATION
L90mm x W90mm x H180mm

Why would only humans make use of eco-friendly technology? OOOMS designed a birdhouse with a solar panel on its roof. During the day, sunlight feeds the solar panel, charging a small battery inside. At twilight, the transparent stick will light up and cast a tiny light on your garden. This light attracts an easy night time snack for the bird; all she has to do is stick her beak out of the hole and wait for the buzz.

Schizo Vase

NAME OF COMPANY | DESIGNER
OOOMS | Guido Ooms & Karin van Lieshout

SPECIFICATION
L490mm x W490mm x H900mm

The word schizophrenia is derived from the Greek words for split (schidzein) and mind (phren). This splitting is related to the fragmentation of the thought processes. OOOMS used this as an inspiration to create a vase with a ribbed surface that creates two different shapes.

The outside shape is based on a Greek Amphora vase. The inner shape is inspired by a brass Indian flower vase. The Schizo Vase is made out of cork, with a transparent finish that makes the vase durable and the inside waterproof.

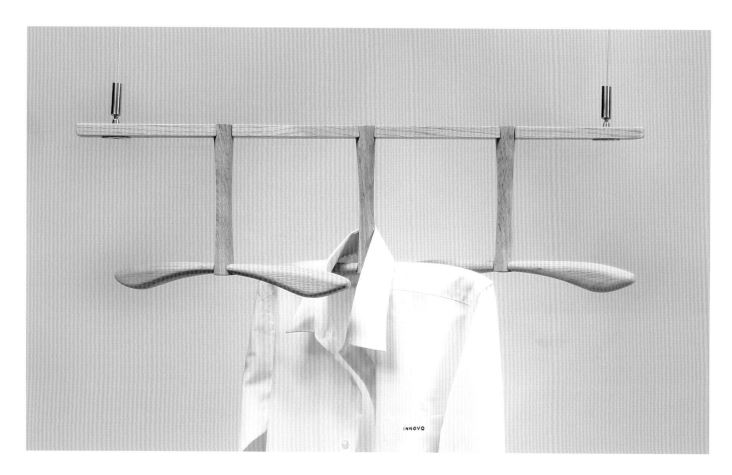

Matching – Shelf

NAME OF COMPANY | DESIGNER
PINWU

SPECIFICATION
D900mm × W300m × H300mm

Matching – Utensil Rack

NAME OF COMPANY | DESIGNER
PINWU

SPECIFICATION
D50mm × W5mm × H40mm

Inspired by the structure of Chinese furniture mortise and tenon joint, the kitchen frame and handle are naturally put together in a concavo-convex positive and negative relationship, with the force of gravity. The joints are mutually restricted, but move in freedom and flexibility. At the end of the handle on each utensil, there is a different thickness that corresponds to its particular place on the utensil rack.

"Fountain" Music Box

NAME OF COMPANY | DESIGNER
BANMOO | Lv Yongzhong

SPECIFICATION
D90mm × W30mm × H30mm

When wound up, these small music boxes make
the sound of trickling fountain water.

"Carrying Moon" Incense Holder

NAME OF COMPANY | DESIGNER
BANMOO | Lv Yongzhong

SPECIFICATION
H170mm × W155mm × D50mm

The outer shape of this piece is a square, while the inner shape is a circle, invoking the image of a full moon. The circle is wider at the bottom and collects the ash from burning incense.

After several days of use, the wood will absorb the scent of the incense, creating a connection between the two.

"Shanghai Man"(left) and "Shanghai Lady"(right) Couple Ring

NAME OF COMPANY | DESIGNER
BANMOO | Lv Yongzhong

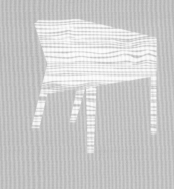

Interviews

FLORIS WUBBEN

Dutch, Interior Design, Product Design, Furniture Design

Awards and Nominations
Ecodesign award 2007 Belgium, Ovam
Portfolio '08, nominated

1.How do you describe your work using only three words?
Nature, craftsman, materials.

2.We all know that material is a crucial element for the designer. Why choose "wood" as a design material?
Wood is a material that offers many creative possibilities; it's also a very interesting looking material. At my Studio we polish the wood so you can see the "wood veins" in its perfect form. But most of the time it's not the designer that chooses the material, but the material that chooses the designer.

3.Some designers believe wood is endowed with wisdom as it is the only material to maintain carbon balance during the whole lifespan. How do you interpret "wood"?
I see wood as a material that we must use with carefulness. Because the use of wood can also form a threat to nature. As a designer I prefer a tree rather than a wooden plank.

4.Which wood product do you prefer? And why?
My Studio uses a lot of willow wood. I really like this material because it's real Dutch wood. It also has beautiful wood veins when you have polished it.

5.Can you share your story about "wood" with us?
The willows in the Netherlands have a lot of moisture and fungus in the fresh wood. Every time we created the chair "Upside down" this was a big problem. So when we created the cabinet "Tree Fungus," we inspired ourselves on this problem and formed it into a structure.

6.How do you interpret the relationship between wood products and environmental protection?
We must never loose our respect for nature. I see it as the responsibility of the designer to show the consumer what is possible with natural friendly wood.

SCOTT JARVIE

Scotland, Product Designer

Jarvie has exhibited at Salone Satellite (Milan), Noise Festival where he won Zaha Hadid's Curators Choice, and 100% Design. Jarvie has worked with Thomas Heatherwick, the internationally acclaimed designer, Elder and Cannon, the innovative award winning Glasgow Architects and Jacki Parry, the renowned Artist and Sculptor.

1.We all know that material is a crucial element for the designer. Why choose "wood" as a design material?
Wood is a unique material – every piece is different. It is warm to touch, robust and easily worked.

2.Some designers believe wood is endowed with wisdom as it is the only material to maintain carbon balance during the whole lifespan. How do you interpret "wood"?
Wood is a renewable resource. But like every natural material we need to use it with intelligence and responsibility. The fact that we can plant more is never a reason to be wasteful. Hardwood is one of the most valuable types of material. It is therefore very important to give great thought to how we intend to use it and endeavour to create something that can be loved for generations.

3.Which wood product do you prefer? And why?
This is a very difficult question. Wood has been used throughout history in our environment and has subsequently had immeasurable effect on our culture.
If I were to choose a single artefact, I think it would be an acoustic guitar. It is a perfect example of a situation where wood is superior to a man-made material in every regard. The combination of the acoustic, structural and aesthetic properties makes wood the perfect choice for the application.
As wood is a natural material, every instrument has a personality of its own.

4.Can you share your story about "wood" with us?
As a child, wood was one of the first materials I worked with. I remember carving faces on the end of sticks to make walking stick handles.
Wood is a wonderful material. Beautiful results can be achieved by a skilled crafts person with only a few humble, inexpensive tools.

5.In China, people believe certain wood can bring good luck. Does "wood" enjoy special meaning in your country?
Wood is a magical material, Witch's Broomsticks are wooden, the Black Pearl Galleon was built from wood and the Wardrobe in The Chronicles of Narnia was also made of wood. So the notion that there is more to wood than its functional attributes is certainly well established in Western culture.

6.How do you interpret the relationship between wood products and environmental protection?
In the future it will be important to make use of all the materials at our disposal in the most sustainable manner, moving away from our disposable consumer culture. I think that wood will play a crucial role in our material future and I hope that we always strive for excellence in design and quality.

RODRIGO BRENNER OF FURF DESIGN STUDIO

Furf Design Studio was born in Curitiba, Brazil, to make people's life more romantic, joyful, poetic and more sensual. Products and interiors are designed with an unusual combination: elegance with irreverence.
Invited to important exhibitions such as the Milan Design Week 2012, 2013 and the Brazilian Design Biennial, Furf has publications around the world. The Brazilian studio even grabbed the attention of Philippe Starck's and Marcel Wanders' Yoo Design Studio, which used one of their products in one of its projects.

1.How do you describe your work using only three words?
Elegant, irreverent, poetic.

2.We all know that material is a crucial element for the designer. Why choose "wood" as a design material?
Just like our fingerprints, every piece of wood is unique: even when mass produced, it is impossible to make two identical products made of this warm material.

3.Some designers believe wood is endowed with wisdom as it is the only material to maintain carbon balance during the whole lifespan. How do you interpret "wood"?
Understanding and respecting this material, we should always push the production processes to their limits to create new forms and functions.

4.Which wood product do you prefer? And why?
Designed by mother-nature, a tree provides you shadow on a sunny day, reduces pollution and could also be used to create a chair, for example. A designer could never design a product with such endless functions.

5.Can you share your story about "wood" with us?
Our first product as Furf Design was the "Verdeamarela chair," with many curves, just like a Brazilian woman. It is completely made of wood. Wood is part of our country and also our own story.

6.In China, people believe certain wood can bring good luck. Does "wood" enjoy special meaning in your country?
When the Portuguese arrived on our land, they were fascinated about our natural resources, especially with the "pau-brasil," a rare tree frequently used to dye noble textiles at that time. That's the reason why our beautiful country is called "Brasil." Since the beginnings of our story, wood has been helping us define our identity.

7.How do you interpret the relationship between wood products and environmental protection?
It reduces the pollution, makes us feel relaxed and it is beautiful, all at the same time. Perfect, isn't it?

AMY HUNTING

Amy Hunting (born 1984) challenges the audience as well as the concept of art in her new project "Faithful Copy" (Tro Kopi) at the RAM Gallery in Oslo. This is also her first solo exhibition. Over the last three years, Hunting has established her own studio in London where she explores the disciplines of design, illustration and drawing. She was invited to exhibit at RAM precisely to draw the lines between these different disciplines in a way that can reveal the way from idea to surface and form.

1.How do you describe your work using only three words?
Honest, simple, with character.

2.We all know that material is a crucial element for the designer. Why choose "wood" as a design material?
Wood is such a basic and primitive material. It's very approachable, and a great starting point for ideas and products. On a practical level, it's a natural resource and easy to get a hold of. It means I can work on it straight away in my workshop and there is no mystery to it.

3.Some designers believe wood is endowed with wisdom as it is the only material to maintain carbon balance during the whole lifespan. How do you interpret "wood"?
I think of wood as a resource which should be used and enjoyed, and it makes many things more beautiful and we should value that.

4.Which wood product do you prefer? And why?
A lot of my works and also furniture at home is wood, and I guess I am surrounded by it.

5.Can you share your story about "wood" with us?
I have a few projects with wood where I have learnt new things about the material and what it can do. The material's properties are important as they give you possibilities and limitations as a designer. I like experimenting with wood in combination with different materials.

6.In China, people believe certain wood can bring good luck. Does "wood" enjoy special meaning in your country?
In Norway, where I am from, we are very much exposed to wood everywhere. We use it to build houses, heat our houses, make furniture etc. Because it's so exposed I think people take it for granted.

7.How do you interpret the relationship between wood products and environmental protection?
I think we should be aware of the impact and use resources that are in abundance and perhaps use more of the more common types of wood.

ORI BEN-ZVI
OF STUDIOUBICO

Israel, Industrial Designer

Operating in the field of sustainable design as an academic and practitioner for the last ten years.

1.How do you describe your work using only three words?
Fine, quirky, designs.

2.We all know that material is a crucial element for the designer. Why choose "wood" as a design material?
Because it's alive and calls for a lot of understanding from the designers' side. It varies in qualities and essence. It is romantic and natural and I find I can identify with those qualities.

3.Some designers believe wood is endowed with wisdom as it is the only material to maintain carbon balance during the whole lifespan. How do you interpret "wood"?
As I work only with reclaimed or recycled wood I would interpret wood as sacred, I hold the strongest respect to it.

4.Which wood product do you prefer? And why?
Cooking accessories. It's a living material for a lively environment.

5.Can you share your story about "wood" with us?
It's a simple material altogether. I fell in love with the material through my first year in design school and ever since have been fascinated with it. I work in other materials as well but when upset or down I go to my workshop and make something, it never failed to work so far.

6.In China, people believe certain wood can bring good luck. Does "wood" enjoy special meaning in your country?
My country has no forests to speak of, what we have are planted pine forests which are quite thin and very few local oak forests which are relatively low. This is part of my interest I would argue, the craving for something I can't have in my home country.

7.How do you interpret the relationship between wood products and environmental protection?
We throw unbelievable quantities of wood while still chopping down ancient forests. It's wrong, so wrong and so sad, as a species we act like children and seem to have no respect to the very beings that create the air we breathe. I think chopping down old trees is dead wrong by itself but doing it while not recycling is a real stupidity.

ZSANETT BENEDEK AND DANIEL LAKOS OF TERVHIVATAL

Hungary, Architectural Designer, Interior Designer, Industrial Designer

1.How do you describe your work using only three words?
Structure, experiment, tenderness.

2.We all know that material is a crucial element for the designer. Why choose "wood" as a design material?
Working with wood comes from our childhood. Our fathers both had small garage-workshops. As we are architects, designing furniture and making wooden models are inherent.

3.Some designers believe wood is endowed with wisdom as it is the only material to maintain carbon balance during the whole lifespan. How do you interpret "wood"?
We like this material because it is sturdy and light at the same time. Its natural character and warm sense is close to us. Even if we paint it white, the nature of wood is present by touch, how it sounds when touching.

4.Which wood product do you prefer? And why?
It depends on purpose. We use thin plywood when we build large surfaces, shells. MDF is a great material for creating solid masses. Genuine hardwood especially with shellac finish is a gorgeous substance radiating the beauty of nature.

5.Can you share your story about "wood" with us?
Whenever we go hunting to flea markets for old furniture parts we feel that they are saving important values from vanishing. The parts we up cycled in the Substitute collection were left on the ground in a crummy paper box. We discovered them instantly and purchased them for 30 Euros. By putting them into the right place gracefulness comes back evidently.

6.In China, people believe certain wood can bring good luck. Does "wood" enjoy special meaning in your country?
Oak is a symbol of state and eternity. On the other hand, as Hungary is a great wine producing country, certain wood types are important for their taste. Oak and Mulberry are popular sources for barrels.

7.How do you interpret the relationship between wood products and environmental protection?
The most important thing is that wooden furniture can survive hundred years. It can be fixed and worth fixing. Wood ages nicely, in contrast to other materials.

JAN GUNNEWEG

The Netherlands, Industrial Designer

Jan Gunneweg is a Dutch designer with a preference for natural products. His greatest passion is wood. Not only because he has built several tree houses during his childhood, but also because of the strength, warmth and flexibility of wood.

The wood designs of Jan Gunneweg are easily accessible by their simplicity and functionality. The products bring people and nature closer together. This is also the motive of Jan Gunneweg, creating more harmony between man and nature.

1.How do you describe your work using only three words?
Happiness by nature!

2.We all know that material is a crucial element for the designer. Why choose "wood" as a design material?
Wood is beautiful; it is a warm and super strong material from nature. The only thing you need is O2 and sunlight and that is infinitely available on Earth.

3.Some designers believe wood is endowed with wisdom as it is the only material to maintain carbon balance during the whole lifespan. How do you interpret "wood"?
Wood absorbs vibration and is silent. If people come into contact with wood, they are friendly, more relaxed and more sociable.

4.Which wood product do you prefer? And why?
All wood types are beautiful because each type of wood has its own properties. Fast-growing wood is weak, but not suitable for construction. Then you use this kind of wood for another project. So you work as a designer on a healthy way with the Earth.

5.Can you share your story about "wood" with us?
Wood has perhaps already experienced a lot and we perhaps not. But you can read some history to the drawing.

6.In China, people believe certain wood can bring good luck. Does "wood" enjoy special meaning in your country?
The Netherlands is another world of timber. We are also known for wooden clogs and windmills.

7.How do you interpret the relationship between wood products and environmental protection?
I think it is very good as people work for a good living environment for both men as animals. My company is also a member of the FSC.

ROSS GARDAM

Australia, Environmental Designer, Interior Designer, Product Designer.

Ross Gardam has worked for a number of large commercial firms in Australia and abroad to develop beautifully simple design solutions to complex problems.

1.How do you describe your work using only three words?
Simple, clean, refined.

2.We all know that material is a crucial element for the designer. Why choose "wood" as a design material?
Wood is an amazingly flexible and adaptable material to use. It can be shaped and formed more easily than many other materials allowing for less restriction in the design process.
Because it is a living material it displays amazing character and patinas with age, ensuring longevity in life.

3.Some designers believe wood is endowed with wisdom as it is the only material to maintain carbon balance during the whole lifespan. How do you interpret "wood"?
I admire the simple beauty of timber, the feel of timber and the history of use.

4.Which wood product do you prefer? And why?
Currently I use a lot of oak as it is readily sustainably available and is a very stable material to work with. The Tasmanian timber species are all individually interesting and display a diverse range of colors, grain and texture.

5.Can you share your story about "wood" with us?
One of my products called Oak is turned from a block of laminated timber and the product always surprises me with new challenges in the manufacturing process. Recently a batch of lights came back with what appeared to be black liquid or dye which had been splashed on the surface. It was a very stubborn stain and very hard to sand back. After much investigation to the source of the stain it was established it was the Tannin in the oak leaching out in the drilling process and oxidising on the surface of the timber. Occurrences such as this continually remind me of the life within the material and there needs to be an allowance in the design and manufacturing for this.

6.In China, people believe certain wood can bring good luck. Does "wood" enjoy special meaning in your country?
Solid timber in Australia is respected as a quality, timeless material and is typically valued in its use and reuse. Recycled and reclaimed timbers are a growing industry in Australia, which reflects not only a respect for the material but a desire to celebrate the life of the timber.

7.How do you interpret the relationship between wood products and environmental protection?

Timber is a precious commodity and should be respected and treated as such. All timbers I use carry an FSC certification and my suppliers have a chain of custody, ensuring all material can be traced back to a sustainably harvested source.

DAVID TRUBRIDGE

New Zealand, Industrial Designer

David Trubridge graduated from Newcastle University in Northern England in 1972 with a degree in Naval Architecture (Boat Design). For the next ten years he lived and worked in rural Northumberland. He taught himself furniture making while working part-time as a forester on a private estate. He went on to develop his own designs which were exhibited around Britain. Many commissions followed, most notably from the Victoria and Albert Museum, St Mary's Cathedral, Edinburgh and the Shipley Galler, Newcastle.

1.How do you describe your work using only three words?
Art, design, craft.

2.We all know that material is a crucial element for the designer. Why choose "wood" as a design material?
It is a material I know intimately because I have worked with wood all my life. I first taught myself the craft skills, and discovered that the wood helps you by quickly telling you when you do something wrong. You can make the same thing again and again in wood, yet every piece is different. It does not require expensive machinery or processes, using low-tech and time-honored processes. It connects us to Nature, bringing Nature into our homes to remind us of its importance to our existence. Wood from sustainably managed plantations is just about the only carbon-positive material.

3.Some designers believe wood is endowed with wisdom as it is the only material to maintain carbon balance during the whole lifespan. How do you interpret "wood"?
I don't endow it with wisdom, which is a human attribute. But I do believe that trees are something we take for granted far too much. They are remarkably complex life-forms which have evolved as an absolutely crucial part of the life-sustaining systems of our planet. Without their water-holding and carbon converting roles, most of our planet would be reduced to a pitiless environment devoid of life as we know it. And yet we persist in stripping our forests! If we take the responsibility, it will be a life-giving resource we can have forever while if we abuse it we will perish.

4.Which wood product do you prefer? And why?
I like solid hardwood from temperate forests, such as ash, oak and elm. These are the timbers I know and which are the easiest to use. Tropical hardwoods often have much more difficult grains and I am very reluctant to use them because too many are illegally logged – even the "legal" ones often have falsified certification. Temperate timbers usually come from well-managed forests in the USA and countries in Europe. Softwoods are too soft for quality, long-lasting

furniture, and are usually not so pleasant to work with. In certain cases I really like plywood – peeling thin veneers off a round log is a very efficient way of converting timber to flat surfaces.

5.Can you share your story about "wood" with us?

Wood made me what I am. It taught me how to make things. It taught me to love and respect our environment. It taught me how to care. When I was learning, I also had a part-time job as a forester on a small private estate in Britain. There I learnt about living trees, how to plant, tend, prune, fell and mill them. One day we dragged an ancient old oak log down to the sawmill. It had lain a long time on the forest floor and was covered in moss and fungi. I was skeptical that this could be of any use to me for furniture. But when we pushed it through the giant spinning blade the two halves rolled apart revealing beautiful, perfect wood grain inside. It was a seminal moment for me which linked the wild unruly forest outside with the furniture in our homes.

6.In China, people believe certain wood can bring good luck. Does "wood" enjoy special meaning in your country?

We have a similar superstitious belief. We say "touch wood" in case something we have said might not come true. It is as if there is a benign tree spirit residing in the dry timber that will look after us. In a sense this is true because of the vital role that trees play in the ecology of Earth. Right now the human race should be saying "touch wood" not to timber, but to our precious living trees.

7.How do you interpret the relationship between wood products and environmental protection?

Wood products from the wrong trees destroy the environment (and hence us). Wood products from the right, sustainably managed trees help protect the environment. They encourage planting and when felled lock up the stored carbon. They can also re-connect us to Nature and hopefully remind us of the importance of caring for it.

LASZLO TOMPA

Hungary, Ceramist, Tile Designer

1996: "Step into the Future" competition, Hungary, first prize (wood furniture)
1999: "Furniture of the Future" competition, Hungary, third prize (wood table)
2000: Competition of the Vasvar city local government in the year of the Millenium, Hungary, "The King's Fountain" (Ceramic fountain)
2004: "Lajos Kozma Craft Fellowship"
2011: IFDA Asahikawa, International Furniture Design Competition, Selected finalist, Japan
IFFT – Interior Life Style Living Exhibition, Tokyo, Japan
2012: Design Exhibition Clerkenwell, London, United Kingdom London Design Festival: Tent London 2012, United Kingdom International Design Exhibition and Fair, MAK, Vienna, Austria Exhibition of Hungarian Studio of Young Designers Association (FISE), Museum of Applied Arts, Budapest

1.How do you describe your work using only three words?
Simple, complicated, clever.

2.We all know that material is a crucial element for the designer. Why choose "wood" as a design material?
I am originally a ceramics and porcelain designer. Recently, my attention turned to tile design. I have been studying tile geometry for years and I have designed a lot of experimental tiles. There was a turning point when I realized that it was possible to use symmetric plane figures to create 3D tile surfaces consisting of bodies of revolution. Further experimenting made it clear that wood would be a much more suitable material to create these shapes. I started designing the other way round: I sought functions for these new, exciting lathed elements joined together. This is how my boxes and suspended lamps were created and I see further possibilities to use them.

3.Some designers believe wood is endowed with wisdom as it is the only material to maintain carbon balance during the whole lifespan. How do you interpret "wood"?
Wood is a magic material: it reacts to environmental conditions sensitively; its annual rings are as communicative as if a journal were read. It unveils the secrets of its growth to us: when weather was favorable and when pollution was higher. We do not know how long forests will be able to counteract the ever increasing harmful impact.

4.Which wood product do you prefer? And why?
Currently, I make boxes and suspended lamps. I like bodies of revolution very much. As we all know, each perpendicular cross-section of these is a circle, which is the most perfect plane figure. I create my objects by chopping and reassembling bodies of

revolution. In the process, a new, complex shape is created by joining simple lathed elements.

5.Can you share your story about "wood" with us?

Both my grandfather and my father were craftsmen who did a lot of wood lathing in their free time. As a child, I was delighted to see them shape wood and create a new object. Throughout several generations in our family, the wood-turning lathe was like a refrigerator in other families. Despite this, I was more attracted by ceramics art. I enjoyed rediscovering wood during the past two years.

6.In China, people believe certain wood can bring good luck. Does "wood" enjoy special meaning in your country?

There is a cute Hungarian custom: people start to make a chair on 13th December, the name-day of Luca. This chair consists of 9 different kinds of timber and 13 pieces. It is forbidden to use nails – the chairs must be assembled using wooden wedges. You can only use one piece a day so it should be finished in 13 days, by the day of Christmas. If you stand on it in the crowd in the church at midnight on 26th December, you can see who has horns because these people are witches.

7.How do you interpret the relationship between wood products and environmental protection?

In Hungary forests are increasing year by year. I think we should strive to use wood – the most important natural material – as much as possible. It is needless to prove its versatility and its excellent properties, and – in contrast with artificial materials – it is very simple to recycle waste wood. It disintegrates within a couple of years in nature and becomes part of the circulation of life again.

DANNY KUO

The Netherlands, Industrial Designer

1.How do you describe your work using only three words?
Functionality, adaptability, fun.

2.We all know that material is a crucial element for the designer. Why choose "wood" as a design material?
In general I enjoy using wood, because it's a warm natural material which is easy to work with. For my Staircase, I chose bamboo, which actually is categorized as a grass, because it's a new material, which is becoming more and more popular. One of the reasons is that it's environmentally friendly, because it grows incredibly fast and in almost any circumstances while as a material has a lot of similar qualities as solid wood.

3.Some designers believe wood is endowed with wisdom as it is the only material to maintain carbon balance during the whole lifespan. How do you interpret "wood"?
I find wood a beautiful natural product, because it is one of the most basic/elemental materials to make products with. I enjoy working with this warm and natural material because it's so close to nature and human basics.

4.Which wood product do you prefer? And why?
I really love bamboo. I first got in touch with bamboo during my internship in Shanghai in 2008. I love it because it's a new material, with new and different looks than wood, but with similar material qualities.

5.How do you interpret the relationship between wood products and environmental protection?
Though there are a lot of problems with rainforests and illegal cutting of trees and the fact that this has a bad influence on nature, I often see incredibly overuse of precious solid woods for furniture pieces. This I don't find responsible. I think designers and manufacturers should keep sustainability and environmental protection in mind when producing and designing their pieces.

FLORIAN KALLUS,
SEBASTIAN SCHNEIDER
OF KASCHKASCH

Germany, Industrial Designer

1.How do you describe your work using only three words?
Simple, honest, smart.

2.We all know that material is a crucial element for the designer. Why choose "wood" as a design material?
Wood makes a special sense when you design things you really touch and use – like a shaft of a hammer for example.

3.Some designers believe wood is endowed with wisdom as it is the only material to maintain carbon balance during the whole lifespan. How do you interpret "wood"?
Wood is a living material which gets ever more beautiful with the years…

4.Which wood product do you prefer? And why?
My favorite wood product is a wooden floor.

5.Can you share your story about "wood" with us?
We both made an apprenticeship as cabinet makers before we became designers – so we really know the material very well. When we were boys we started working with wood and what we always loved was the character of the surface and the smell of the material and it's the same today. It's a warm material with soul.

6.In China, people believe certain wood can bring good luck. Does "wood" enjoy special meaning in your country?
In Germany, they use the word "wood" for money… There are also sayings such as"knock on wood" and so on…

NIC WEBB

UK, Industrial Designer

1.How do you describe your work using only three words?
Simple and thoughtful.

2.We all know that material is a crucial element for the designer. Why choose "wood" as a design material?
Greenwood is a pliable material that twists, changes color and can be formed as it seasons. When working, the hand and mind respond to the grain of the wood and designs follow spontaneously. This offers great freedom in the making process and delivers wonderful natural surprises.

3.Some designers believe wood is endowed with wisdom as it is the only material to maintain carbon balance during the whole lifespan. How do you interpret "wood"?
Wood is pure and organic. When working with wood one connects with the natural world and the history of human making. Wood does not need to be wise. Only people need to be wise.

4.Which wood product do you prefer? And why?
The Tree. Its possibilities are endless.

5.Can you share your story about "wood" with us?
My Great, Great Grandfather, Job Andrews was a woodsman working in the South of England. My Great Grandfather, Grandfather and Father were all solicitors but they carried through their lives their Father's chest of tools. When my Father died I

inherited the tools of my Great, Great Grandfather and they are now the backbone of my work. One day these tools will be passed to the next generation.

6.In China, people believe certain wood can bring good luck. Does "wood" enjoy special meaning in your country?

Woods and the Forests have many meanings in Britain. Trees and their woods can symbolize the differences of Men and Women and the connection between humans and the natural world. Wood is integral to all our lives.

7.How do you interpret the relationship between wood products and environmental protection?

There is environmental impact in all making but working with natural materials that are sourced in a sustainable manner and worked with low energy traditional hand tools is as gentle as any maker can hope to be.

I work predominantly with greenwood and combine stone, metal, ceramic and paint in my work. Using both traditional and modern tools as well as elemental forces such as fire and ice, I produce handcrafted objects of art and design.

Through my work I explore the value and symbolism associated with objects of simple function, the materials from which they are made and the integral connection between human creation and the natural world.

ROBERTO OF WEWOOD

Italy, Industrial Designer

1.How do you describe your work using only three words?
Fashionable, sustainable, eco-conscious.

2.We all know that material is a crucial element for the designer. Why choose "wood" as a design material?
The beauty of the grain gives our watches a uniqueness that is desired. We feel the wood accessory brings us closer to nature.

3.Some designers believe wood is endowed with wisdom as it is the only material to maintain carbon balance during the whole lifespan. How do you interpret "wood"?
Wood is nature. We strive to respect that and plant a tree for each watch sold.

4.Which wood product do you prefer? And why?
We prefer to use recycled or mostly reclaimed wood. This way we further reduce our impact on our planet.

5.Can you share your story about "wood" with us?
WEWOOD was born in Florence, Italy by three entrepreneurs who share both a love of watches and the environment. WEWOOD is a brand that came out of the necessity to create a beautiful accessory that stands out and a commitment to find a sustainable way to do business, which is very important in the time we live in. We are aware of the social commitment and the environmental message behind our products; which is why we decided to create something that gives back to nature more than we are taking away.

6.In China, people believe certain wood can bring good luck. Does "wood" enjoy special meaning in your country?
In a time when synthetic materials make the majority of products, wood is a reminder of nature.

7.How do you interpret the relationship between wood products and environmental protection?
Wood is natural and beautiful and its origin must be respected. There is a way to balance what is taken from our planet and what is given. WEWOOD is delighted to have teamed up with Trees For The Future, by planting 120,000 trees together so far just from our American office. We are looking forward to the continued partnership maintaining our commitment to plant one tree for every watch sold.

ELISA HONKANEN

Finland, Industrial Designer

Coming from Finland Elisa Honkanen has learned from the very beginning to appreciate the pure and practical lifestyle. In design this means continuous self-analyzing: questioning if the object is truly needed and honesty to oneself in evaluting the project.

1.We all know that material is a crucial element for the designer. Why choose "wood" as a design material?
I like using wood as it gives warmth for the objects. It is pleasant to touch and brings a presence of nature in our "high-tech" environment. I think that as the world is getting more and more "high tech," natural materials get more precious as they give us the sensation of staying connected to nature.

2.Some designers believe wood is endowed with wisdom as it is the only material to maintain carbon balance during the whole lifespan. How do you interpret "wood"?
For me wood is a noble material, it brings a touch of uniqueness in the objects as the wood grain is always different.

3.Which wood product do you prefer? And why?
My favorite woods are birch and oak. I love the grain markings in oak and birch. They are beautiful light hardwoods. (They are also traditional woods in Finland, so they remind of my home.)

4.Can you share your story about "wood" with us?
My story of wood would probably go back to my childhood and memories of skiing in a forest of high spruce branches covered with usnea.

5.In China, people believe certain wood can bring good luck. Does "wood" enjoy special meaning in your country?
Traditionally we had holy trees and we have had lots of deities associated in trees. In the countryside it was common to have a tree protecting the house (when a new house was built one tree was chosen from proximity of the house and protected with care. The tree had to be younger than the builder; otherwise it wouldn't respect and protect the owner of the house and his family). I think everyone can sense the majestic atmosphere in an old forest; it is almost a kind of religious experience.

6.How do you interpret the relationship between wood products and environmental protection?
I think wood is already regarded as a high value material in the furniture industry, and I think there is a good reason to continue using wood in furniture as it will always remind us of nature simply with its presence. But naturally the wood production should be done in a way as sustainable as possible, respecting the environment until the very end.

KLARA SUMOVA

Czech Republic, Independent Product and Interior Designer

Klára is an independent product and interior designer based in Prague, with works extending to the northern Czech Republic.

1.How do you describe your work using only three words?
Interest, materials, process (and love)!

2.We all know that material is a crucial element for the designer. Why choose "wood" as a design material?
I think the wood found me. My first project made out of wood was "Lamp Love." Initially, I wanted to produce the lamp out of paper, but my research led me to wood. This material showed me lots of new techniques, but I didn't know enough about woodworking. And this fact influenced the final design. Since then I've gained more knowledge about working with wood. I realized that I was quite naively brave to make the lamp out of raw wood. But after that, all my projects have contained wood.

3.Some designers believe wood is endowed with wisdom as it is the only material to maintain carbon balance during the whole lifespan. How do you interpret "wood"?
For me, wood is a beautiful, natural material, which gives a lot of options of how to work with it. The fact that it is a material which is nature friendly is a big plus in my work – I like to research materials and produce locally and sustainably. The first moment I fell in love with wood was while researching its structure and behaviour. I like to combine elements of the wood's natural state with those of the manufacturing and woodworking processes. Just observing wood still gives me inspiration.

4.Which wood product do you prefer? And why?
My favorite is actually my first project – "Lamp Love." I like it because it is a lovely project, it is still in producion and keeps finding people – who are very happy to have it in their homes. And I

like that the idea is clear and talks to people.

5.Can you share your story about "wood" with us?
When I said that "Lamp Love" was my first wood project – I meant professional wood project. My first memory of wood occured a long time before that. I always adored the little wooden horse my father made as a kid, which is displayed at my parents' house. The fact that he had his own workshop and was building furniture made me feel that everything is possible to produce – from the big scale to the small one.

6.In China, people believe certain wood can bring good luck. Does "wood" enjoy special meaning in your country?
Nothing specific comes to mind, but Czech Republic is a country with big forestry and a really beautiful cottage culture. Lots of people are interested in refining wood, making their own little summer houses and decorating them. So I naturally tend to share this mood.

7.How do you interpret the relationship between wood products and environmental protection?
I like that wood has a lot of different faces. It can look like a precious gem or all the dust and leftovers may be part of various composites or construction materials. Wood is incredible by its behaviour and it is part of nature – just as it grows, it can also dissapear. Forests are a pleasure to be in and the same pleasure can be found when surrounded by wood at home. Individuals should definitely consider the environment in their daily routines.

WU WEI

China, Industrial Designer

Germany Red Dot design award winner; Original design director of Peking University Founder Group Co., Ltd.; Former graduate project guidance of Royal College of Art in United Kingdom. In late 2010, he set up Thru creative institution which aims at designing and making original furniture and household products. In 2011 he established Thruwood training to systematically disseminate woodworking knowledge and skills to the public.

1.How do you describe your work using only three words?
Tranquility, happy, thankful.

2.We all know that material is a crucial element for the designer. Why choose "wood" as a design material?
Wooden furniture represents a tradition. The reason for my choosing pure solid wood is that I love making wood furniture by hand. Different timbers have different personalities and differ in color, smell, grain and quality, which provide great space for designers.

3.Some designers believe wood is endowed with wisdom as it is the only material to maintain carbon balance during the whole lifespan. How do you interpret "wood"?
Besides the environmental protection property as a carbon-holding material, wood has a special meaning to designers. Although they are all woods, there are a lot of wood types and every type has its own unique inherence and appearance. Excellent furniture design requires designers to combine their own emotions with material, and to cherish and think carefully of wood, so as to make wood radiate its unique beautiful temperament.

4.Which wood product do you prefer? And why?
My favorite one is "Little Tree Chair," because the raw materials for making it are waste wood. First off cut is used to create the back and seat, and then depending on its existing temperament, dead

tree trunks are used to make chair legs, which results in a new vigor. Therefore, this work has a unique vitality. My favorite series is Mingxin wood furniture produced by Thru, which perfectly interprets Thru designers' understanding of modern Chinese style.

5.Can you share your story about "wood" with us?

I liked trees from childhood, the fresh breath trees give off and the unique feelings of bare branches swaying in the cold wind in winter. I also like all kinds of wooden furniture. A dozen years ago when I just worked, I faintly felt I would do some wood-related design work. Then I began my woodworking. Over one and a half years ago I created "Thru" – the brand of original solid wood furniture and developed woodworking training camps to disseminate woodworking courses of traditional furniture the social masses. Now it may be assumed that all of this has its own fate, but working with wood was destined for me.

6.In China, people believe certain wood can bring good luck. Does "wood" enjoy special meaning in your country?

Wood is my favorite material. I always feel joyful in the course of working with wood, therefore wood is very special to me. And in China, wood has been penetrating deeply into our traditional culture. For example, when talking about seasons, wood represents spring, growth and development, and gives us a positive feeling.

Index

Lotte van Laatum
http://www.lottevanlaatum.nl

Markus Johansson
http://markusjohansson.com

MOISSUE
http://moissue.com

MORELESS
www.more-less.com.cn

Nic Webb
www.nicwebb.com

OOOMS
www.oooms.nl

Pavel Eekra
http://eekra.com

PINWU
www.pinwu.net

Ross Gardam
http://rossgardam.com.au

Scoops Design
http://scoopsdesign.bigcartel.com

Scott Jarvie
http://www.scottjarvie.co.uk

SmartwoodHouse
www.smartwoodhouse.com

STUDIO MAKKINK & BEY
www.studiomakkinkbey.nl

Studio ubico
http://www.studioubico.com

StudioKahn
www.studiokahn.com

Tal Gur
http://www.talgur.com

Tervhivata
lhttp://www.tervhivatal.hu

Thru
www.thruwood.com

Thomas Schnur
http://www.thomasschnur.com

Vyrobeno Lesem
www.vyrobenolesem.com

WEWOOD
http://we-wood.us

zizaoshe
www.zizaoshe.com